LIT FROM INSIDE

LIT FROM INSIDE

40 YEARS OF POETRY FROM

ALICE JAMES BOOKS

EDITED BY

ANNE MARIE MACARI & CAREY SALERNO

FOREWORD BY

MAXINE KUMIN

Alice James Books

FARMINGTON, MAINE

www.alicejamesbooks.org

10 9 8 7 6 5 4 3 2 1

Alice James Books are published by Alice James Poetry Cooperative, Inc., an affiliate of
the University of Maine at Farmington.

Alice James Books
238 Main Street
Farmington, ME 04938
www.alicejamesbooks.org

Library of Congress Cataloging-in-Publication Data

Lit from inside : 40 years of poetry from Alice James Books / edited by Anne Marie
Macari, Carey Salerno ; introduction by Maxine Kumin.
    p. cm.
  Includes bibliographical references and index.
  ISBN 978-1-882295-96-8 (pbk.)
  1. American poetry. 2. Publishers and publishing--History. 3. Alice James
Books. I. Macari, Anne Marie. II. Salerno, Carey.
  PS586.L54 2013
  811.008--dc23
                        2012029641

Alice James Books gratefully acknowledges support from individual donors, private
foundations, the University of Maine at Farmington, and the National Endowment for
the Arts.

ART WORKS.
arts.gov

Cover art work by E.V. Day, *SEDUCERS II*, 2010-11, Published by Carolina Nitsch.

TABLE OF CONTENTS

ACKNOWLEDGMENTS

Alice James Books wishes to thank our boards, our "Alices," and our many staff and directors over the last forty years. We have made a partial list but we can't list everyone who has served on the board or who has promoted and given time and dedication to the press, so please know that if we do not mention your name, we have not forgotten your gifts of poetry and time and belief in AJB. Here is an incomplete list of people we want to mention and thank, without whom the press might long ago have folded:

Patricia Cumming, Marjorie Fletcher, Jean Pedrick, Lee Rudolph, Ron Schreiber, Betsy Sholl, Cornelia Veenendaal, Marie Harris, Beatrice Hawley, Kinereth Gensler, Celia Gilbert, Ruth Buchman, Jane Kenyon, Jean Valentine, Suzanne Matson, Ellen Doré Watson, Peg Peoples, April Ossmann, Aimee Beale, Amy Dryansky, Peter Waldor, Judy Swahnberg, Jean Amaral, Theo Kalikow, David Harvey, Allen Berger, Wesley McNair, Jeffrey Thomson.

A very special thanks as well to our amazing research assistants, Shawn Callahan and Kate Thompson, who worked diligently and deftly to aid us with all the minutia of putting together this great work. And to Meg Willing, an enormous helping of gratitude: your meticulous eye and dedication to this "tome" is so appreciated. We could not have put this book together without you.

FOREWORD

F orty years old and flourishing—a remarkable record for a small nonprofit press—Alice James Books deserves praise and admiration. Founded in 1973 as a cooperative press by seven idealists—five women and two men, all of whom are represented herein—their stated goal, to involve the poets themselves in the publishing process, and to provide a venue for women at a time when such access to publication was extremely limited, has been handsomely fulfilled. (Men are also represented, though in small numbers.) The press takes its name from Alice James, the sister of luminaries William and Henry, whose own gifts went unremarked in her lifetime.

Alice James Books has remained a cooperative. It sponsors two annual book competitions: the Beatrice Hawley Award and the Kinereth Gensler Awards, whose winners are named to the cooperative board and take part in selecting ensuing collections. The Kundiman Poetry Prize, open to all Asian American poets with any number of published books, was inaugurated in 2010 and the AJB Translation Series preceded it in 2008.

Arranged chronologically, the list of authors is remarkable for its breadth, variety, and passion. This is a big book: a reader needs fortitude to undertake its 200+ pages, but anthologies are meant to be sipped, not gulped thirstily. Nevertheless, in gradual and measured swallows, I have downed the entire collection, 130-odd disparate celebratory, elegiac, lyrical, lofty, comic, surreal, imagist, formalist, postmodern bards. The assortment is idiosyncratic; the range of voices and styles embraces the familiar personal narrative voice and the innovative, often dissonant music of more experimental poets.

It has been pointed out that the poet's vocation is in itself a declaration of independence. It has, as Stanley Kunitz once remarked, no market value. Hence, it is all but incorruptible. This anthology owes allegiance to none, other than the poets who have been selected by the cooperative board. Ed Ochester, introducing a forty-year anthology of University of Pittsburgh poets, sagely described the university and small independent presses as "the garage bands of the publishing industry."

Now let us strike up the music. What could be more incongruent than the juxtaposition of seriocomic, irreverent, loquacious David Kirby with his long narrative line and lyrical, elliptical poet of brevity, Jane Mead? Thanks to their coincident publication dates, Kirby's *The Temple Gate Called Beautiful* (2008) and Mead's *The Usable Field* of the same year, they abut in the table of contents. Kirby's title poem opens:

> It says HELL IS HOT HOT HOT HOT
> and NO SEX WITH MEN ALOUD
> and NO ICE WATER IN HELL
> on the hundreds of washers and dryers
> and air conditioner housings that stud
> the land around outsider artist W.C. Rice's house. . .

And Mead's "The Origin"—the title runs right into the poem:

> of what happened is not in language—
> of this much I am certain.
> Six degrees south, six east—
>
> and you have it: the bird
> with the blue feathers, the brown bird—
> same white breasts. . .

On to elegiac poems—isn't all poetry elegiac *au fond*? All poems are rooted in the mortality we bemoan; if we were immortal we would have no need to record human feelings in poetry. So many poems here moved me, but none more profoundly than Kathleen Sheeder Bonanno, whose poems about the murder of her daughter that gave rise to *Slamming Open the Door,* are masterly. The title poem opens:

> In his Russian greatcoat,
> slamming open the door
> with an unpardonable bang,
> and he has been here ever since.

and concludes:

> Even as I sit here,
> he stands behind me
> clamping two
> colossal hands on my shoulders
> and bends down
> and whispers to my neck:
> *From now on,*
> *you write about me.*

Other elegies I found notable include "Washing Beans" by Rita Gabis; E.J. Miller Laino's poem, "No Stone;" Catherine Barnett's "The Disbelieving," and David Williams's "Available Light."

And what would an anthology be without some poems about poets writing poems? Here are four: "Lowell Reading" by John Hildebidle; "Wait" by Susan Snively; "To Plath, to Sexton" by Jean Valentine, and Lee Rudolph's "The Fireman's Ball," a hilarious plea for poets to pressure the public the way firefighters do as they hawk tickets to their dance:

> . . . does anyone
> admire the poets' long brass stanzas,
> their black, pliant, waterproof metaphors. . . ?

Poems about family and poems about relationships abound. In the ironically titled "Father's Day," Suzanne Matson describes

[o]ne father, mine, sits far away and waits to die, mumbling
old grudges to his tireless self. . . .
. . . .
he sits

pissed off and bony, a gray silt of whiskers
and wild brows and flaking skin. . . .
. . . .
But let us not dwell
on that. Let us dwell on the rhythmic ringing notes

of his hammer in the backyard thirty years ago
. . . .

. . . And everything was green:
the big house, the little house, the backyard and our tightly
furled lives.

Miriam Goodman's "Argument for Parting" ends "And I don't marry.
/ I don't buy land. / I get older by myself" and Tom Absher's "The
Hermit" closes with "Winter and I have a talent for emptiness— /
this is going to be a sweet exile." These two poets suggest the rejection of earlier relationships and the acceptance of an independent hermetic life. Ellen Doré Watson's "One of the Ones" and Frank X. Gaspar's "One Thousand Blossoms" seem to be cries from the heart; Watson writes:

I won't forget you and you and you, each
with a brutal truth to send away
in a little boat, let me be one of the ones
to keep it afloat. . .

Gaspar declares, "You don't want less love—this ground has been
covered before— / you want more love, even when you can't say what it
means."

In "Prairie" Robin Becker describes

[t]wo women in a field
in the middle of our lives,
while the whole wrecked world
slides into tomorrow.
Her hands come to my body and I would rest
in that simplicity. This field this night. . .

Poems about war deserve more space than I can allot them here. Both Doug Anderson, author of *The Moon Reflected Fire* and Brian Turner, of *Here, Bullet,* have seen combat and their poems have been wrung from it. In "Short Timer" Anderson reports:

I syringed the long gash. . . with sterile water. . .
. . . .
the man saying, *Oh God,* and already the slur,
the drool. . .
. . . .
What was in the 20 cc's of brain he lost?

Turner's title poem arrests us with

And I dare you to finish
what you've started. Because here, Bullet,
here is where I complete the word you bring
hissing through the air, here is where I moan
the barrel's cold esophagus, triggering
my tongue's explosives

Theodore Deppe, formerly a nurse, writes in "The Book of God" about the photo of a crucified girl, "one of several Bosnian children nailed to the doors / of their own homes to frighten the parents away." These poets have excoriating tales to tell; we need to listen.

Three poets—Kazim Ali, Anne Marie Macari, and Henrietta Goodman—are represented here with poems about faith. Ali, a Muslim, writes about the Hagar and Ismael story. Macari cites Mary and Luke. Goodman states,

> God as an engine seems right. Not God
> to make promises to, or in front of,
>
> but God to grind promises up,
>
> burn them like gas.

B.H. Fairchild's "Keats," is a memorable poem that deserves mention. It opens:

> I knew him. He ran the lathe next to mine.
> Perfectionist, a madman, even on overtime. . .
> . . . .
>
> and I remember the red hair flaming
> beneath the lamp, calipers measuring out
> the last cut, his hands flicking iron burrs
> like shooting stars through the shadows.

One dream poem startled me. (I am sure there are others, but nothing quite so dramatic.) It is a persona poem from *Night Watches: Inventions on the Life of Maria Mitchell*, Carole Oles's collection about the mid-nineteenth century American woman astronomer. Full of foreboding about her reception in academia, Mitchell dreams,

> I am delivered to Harvard
> in a black carriage with curtains
>
> The lecture hall churns
> . . . .

I open my mouth to begin
and my teeth spill out
powdery as chalk

Dear reader, I've been there; possibly some of you have, too.

In addition to finding widely diverging thematic concerns, I searched for varying prosodic approaches. I needed to look no further than the first poem in the collection, "Mallard" by Cornelia Veenendaal for the ballast of metaphor. The bird is "a pilot of the inland waters"; he uses his "brilliant paddles" during migration to "row over whole states. . . ."

Many poets use stanza breaks to shift time or place or mood. Linnea Johnson moves from her own "crosscut handsaw" to "yours" in the second stanza, then leaps to "I am in love with you from the neck down" in the third.

And then there is the deliberate density of lines that do not invite scansion but run pell-mell without punctuation, capitalizing the first letter of each line to lend the poem a formal aspect. See Matthea Harvey's "In Defense of Our Overgrown Garden."

Anaphora, caesura, internal rhymes, the sound effects of alliteration, assonance, and consonance all add varying tonalities.

There are two prose poems, a scant handful of poems in rhyme, an acute shortage of sonnets, villanelles, and sestinas. Perhaps this is not surprising in an anthology of contemporary poets; perhaps it is a tribute to the variety and skill of the poems that this unregenerate old formalist can say she enjoyed this assignment.

—MAXINE KUMIN

EDITOR'S PREFACE

40 Years Later: Alice James Books

In 1973, when Alice James Books came into being, there were few small presses; young poets struggling to write outside of the mainstream, to find distinctive voices, women writers struggling to be accepted, often found themselves up against a tightly guarded literary world. It's worth a glance back to see what was happening in our culture forty years ago. Certainly 1973 marked a moment when the women's movement was at its height: it was the year Adrienne Rich published *Diving into the Wreck*, and the year Roe vs. Wade made abortion a constitutional right. It was the year the Paris Peace Accords were signed and the Watergate hearings began.

The birth of a small poetry press, a cooperative and self-made venture, might seem insignificant in light of those events, but AJB is representative of the kind of shift in the poetry world that has deepened and taken hold in the forty years since the press was started. From the founding of more writing programs, to the founding of small presses, there has been an explosion in poetry. Not just more poets, but more diversity; even if poetry remains a fairly marginal activity, the last forty years have seen the democratization of poetry, more students with access to writing programs, more publishers, more first books. Poetry is no longer an elite activity for a small group of established and anointed poets.

In 1973 the seven founders of Alice James Books—Patricia Cumming, Marjorie Fletcher, Jean Pedrick, Lee Rudolph, Ron Schreiber, Betsy Sholl, and Cornelia Veenendaal—were part of an ongoing poetry workshop energized by weekly meetings as well as group readings that attracted many listeners and poets from around the Boston area. They clearly were inspired by their work together, but there was one frustration they shared: they were consistently rejected by publishers and magazines. The messages that came to the women were particularly discouraging. It's hard to believe now that a publisher could say, "You write too much like a woman," but this kind of rejection was not so uncommon. Even women who were successfully publishing and winning attention and awards were scrutinized and critiqued in ways that marginalized and stigmatized their work. Here, Maxine Kumin writes about the book reviews of her friend and colleague Anne Sexton:

> . . .years before he wrote his best-selling novel, *Deliverance*, which centers on a graphic scene of homosexual rape, James Dickey, writing in the *New York Times Book Review*, excoriated the poems in *All My Pretty Ones*, saying, "It would be hard to find a writer who dwells more insistently on the pathetic and disgusting aspects of bodily experience. . .
>
> (Anne Sexton, *The Complete Poems*)

Women who didn't want to write in polite code, who didn't want to *write like a man*, came up against entrenched and privileged power in the form of editors, publishers, and critics. Though the problem was particularly acute for women who were being sent mixed messages about how they should write and what they should write about, women weren't the only ones struggling to see themselves in print.

It was a brave and wild leap of faith to start a press without money or backing, with just the sense that something was wrong in the poetry world and the way to help make it right was to give "power to women and power to authors." The new press was feminist but didn't exclude men, as is obvious by the fact that two of the founders were men. Jean Valentine got a call from one of the early members inviting her to be an advisor to the press. Jean asked, "Will you be publishing any men?" "Of course!" Later the same call was made to Adrienne Rich who asked, "Will you be publishing any men?" "Of course not!" The nascent publishers were not just brave, they knew how to hedge their bets.

AJB's founders published its first books by doing it all themselves—from design, to the editing process, to production. The press was established as a collective; authors were expected to work at the press. In the beginning there was no staff, just authors volunteering their time. It worked because in those first years they only accepted authors from New England who would be close enough to be able to help out. Little by little the press brought in part time staff and cobbled together finances through small grants and book sales. Some board members served out their time and left, others stayed on as volunteers for many years. No one person, no one group of people, is responsible for AJB's survival. Collectively, authors and staff have built the press year by year. If bringing in new board members each year has kept a degree of uncertainty alive at AJB, it has also brought diversity and energy to the press. Working by consensus the board might fight it out over manuscripts, but eventually the various members come together.

In 1986, after the death of Beatrice Hawley, an early author and member of the cooperative board, a national award was established in her name so that AJB could begin to accept books outside the New England area by authors who would not have to be on the board and work for the press. This marked an important milestone: finally poets from all over the country could be published by AJB.

From the time of the founding of AJB, money had been an issue. Even when the books were selling—and they did sell—there were years it looked like financial difficulties would bring an end to it all. Finally, after twenty years of operation, Alice James Books became affiliated with the University of Maine at Farmington which gave the press some long awaited stability, as well as a home. In a symbiotic exchange, UMF provides services such as housing, equipment, and funding, while AJB benefits the University with its presence in support of the school's creative writing program. The press provides professional experience and educational opportunities for many students each year and strengthens the state school's reputation as a major leader in creative writing and liberal arts.

But AJB's most important assets have always been its authors and their books. Though some of those authors have given years of their time to serve the press, the overall mission has always been about the poetry. We've looked for beautiful books, important books, books that might not other-wise find a home. AJB published Jane Kenyon's first book, *From Room to Room*, and two volumes of Jean Valentine's poems, including *Home. Deep. Blue: New and Selected Poems*. We published Doug Anderson's *The Moon Reflected Fire*, poems of the war in Vietnam, as well as the first poems to come out of the war in Iraq, *Here, Bullet*, by Brian Turner. When B. H. Fairchild sent his manuscript, *The Art of the Lathe*, to the Beatrice Haw-ley Award, it had been rejected everywhere else and he had decided that the AJB contest would be the last time he'd send it out. Fairchild's book went on to gain much attention and was nominated for the National Book Award.

There is a long list of people who have kept AJB alive, well, and grow-ing. From the many board members to the executive directors, to our list of donors and staff, the press has survived and grown far beyond the early vision of the seven founders. In 2011 the press published the first book in its translation series, *Hagar Before the Occupation | Hagar After the Occupation*, by Amal al-Jubouri, translated by Rebecca Gayle Howell and Husam Qaisi, a stunning book that gives us a view of the Iraq War from an Iraqi woman living in exile. That same year saw the publication of *Pier* by Janine Oshiro, the first book published in collaboration with Kundiman, an organization that promotes and nurtures Asian American poetry.

For this anthology, Carey Salerno, AJB's executive director, and I, read every book AJB has published in its forty years. Each and every author through 2012 is represented here. Though we shared all the reading, Carey did much of the heavy lifting for this volume, searching the files for inter-esting archival material, and handling the details of design and permissions, among other things. I have to say that sitting in my dining room with all the books in piles around us was a bit paralyzing at first. But over the course of a few days we found that we agreed on most of the poems. When we weren't sure about someone's work, we'd read it out loud and that turned out to be incredibly helpful. We could hear what we often couldn't discern on the page. We came to enjoy hearing the poems so much that we read aloud quite a bit. Even poems we were sure of took us by surprise when read aloud. I remember reading Theodore Deppe's moving poems, Cecilia Gilbert's, Catherine Barnett's, and Kevin Goodan's, among others.

Alice James Books began simply and organically, a small writing group who encouraged each other, who set out to see each other's work into print and then continued to expand their vision. Forty years later, AJB has become an important press. The goals haven't changed, there will always be marginalized voices, and so AJB has kept questioning itself, widening its gaze, not wanting to become too comfortable in its own skin. We remain a cooperative, nonprofit press that depends not only on its members, but on outside funding and donors to keep afloat. We hold onto our original feminist goals. In a time of financial uncertainty and huge changes in publishing, we are still here, still publishing what we believe are necessary books, books that are beautiful to look at and hold in a time when the e-book is surging in popularity and our collective culture is bouncing off our ubiquitous electronic screens. We all multitask and seem to work constantly, but I'm not sure how much we are actually getting done. Poetry couldn't be more important now. To sit quietly with a book, to leave the surface and dive under, may very soon seem like a radical activity. I hope Alice James Books will continue to be around for many more years, helping us hear those under-voices, bringing vitality and depth to our readers.

—ANNE MARIE MACARI

LIT FROM INSIDE

The Mallard

CORNELIA VEENENDAAL

To be a pilot of the inland waters and the air
he has become a form touchingly subtle
and wears a shirt of fat where
he is diamonded with seven sober colors.
Setting forth he turns his brilliant paddles,
or floats in icy ponds. In the heights
of his migration he rows over whole states.
In reedy shadows summer nights
he gives his plainspeech criticism,
flaps open iridescent plans.
The mallard is for happiness in marriage;
no breach in his body or in his habits
lets trauma drive its wedge.

Taken from *The Trans-Siberian Railway*

Minority Report

CORNELIA VEENENDAAL

At 6 A.M.
sparrows!

Along the high flat cornices
and in the spine of the street
their speech
riddles the air.

A child in a window
yawns a dark O.

At the steep ascent of waking
to cry out sharply

I do not agree!
I do not agree!

Taken from *Green Shaded Lamps*

In Reply to Letters of Condolence

PATRICIA CUMMING

Don't only praise him after he's dead.
He once could change and was not always

as certain.
Be as quiet as though he was living.
But those who break and need sun.
Also praise them.

Taken from *Afterwards*

Drawing Lesson

PATRICIA CUMMING

Half an inch
high, you stand (cheerfully,
alive), a long
way away

in the upper left
corner of the picture.
I can barely
see your face. But the roads,

the rivers all run
to you, the trees, the horizon
point to you, the sun the sky
shines on you: I

am learning perspective.

Taken from *Afterwards*

poem reluctantly written at quarter of four in the morning
KAREN LINDSEY

if el greco had known me
he would have given me the view of toledo.
say he'd been handsome, and we were lovers.
or pals, anyway, moving in the same crowds.
if you like it so much, he'd have said, take it.
i, of course, moon-eyed, refusing,
finally accepting—
and long after we'd lost touch,
i'd have it, on a wall in a little, dark room
all my own
and all the time looking, looking at it
till a day came
when the dark, raincloud road turning off the right
would slither from the picture,
trail down to the floor,
smooth itself under my feet
and off, off i'd go,
soft, into toledo
and nothing changed in the picture,
no new figure, tiny on the road,
no face looking from a hidden graywhite window
back
on an old, gone world

Taken from *Falling Off the Roof*

Snow Moon

JEAN PEDRICK

There is a stretch of prairie in the mind,
one little frontier more. Our city hulks
around us in a creaking ring; it is
a caravan stopped; the wheeling chimneys
whinny; snow drives like a dust storm
into all the rifts between our needs.

I say to the fire: *Make me warm.*
You say to the nurse with the pills:
What good will they do?

All prairie ripples between, a virgin field
where not so much as a rabbit's foot kicks up
track from a life. Deserted silences
swallow our several echoes — hunger, anger

Taken from *Wolf Moon*

Great Swelling Things

JEAN PEDRICK

for Anne and Richard

Remember sleeping there,
far from all edges in the brass bed,
the copious maples making
shadows of wild applause on the wall?
In the next room the comic opera
of their sleep-duet, miles down
in mountain meadow featherbeds?

Remember her shout: *Um Gottes Willen*
when she reaches the kitchen door
and meets the dough too risen, grown
down the sides of the bowl, acrawl
on the table—alive, alive!

Repicture how he shaves, his
cup-and-mirror on the kitchen window,
carefully wraps his four-in-hand, pats on
his suit coat, dons his Panama and strolls
three blocks to buy a 3¢ cake of yeast
as though formality will this time tame it?

Taken from *Pride & Splendor*

home from our fathers

R O N S C H R E I B E R

for Tom

six at dinner when the phone rang,
you were half-finished. I put
a piece of meat in my mouth & listened.
"I think it's his mother," Mary said.

your mother called to tell you that
your father died in Florida
on the golf course, just as his
father died—an American death,
watching the pros & never breaking par.

my father in Florida was seventy last week,
the youngest of seven. he's healthy there.
his brother & his sisters are still living,
except for his oldest sister, who died
of flu in the twenties.

it's you I care about. last night
I wanted to comfort you, to sleep with you
not because of death but because
I want to sleep with you again.
today you're in Pontiac comforting your mother,
attending to funeral details.
I missed you when you were in New Hampshire.
I miss you now.

we have a home here, we're making a family
far from our parents' houses, lined up
in rows on similar streets
like those men in identical raincoats
at the airport when you left.

                         our fathers were
confused. to be fathers meant to want to love
& not know how. they weren't chameleons,
could not change colors between home & office
though they knew gray wasn't bright enough.

your father has suffered
a sea change now.
come back home.

Taken from *Moving to a New Place*

After Reading Bashō

BETSY SHOLL

I dream of a terrible journey
with rivers named *parents-desert-*
children, or *children-desert-parents*,
with mountains named *all-wealth-*
is-useless, with steep mountain trails
named *end-of-desire*, named *all-you-*
may-care-for-are-shrines.

I dream of a terrible journey
with roads named *end-of-ability-*
to-choose, with roads named
ability-to-choose-end forking out
in every direction, dense, hung with
branches and vines named *horses-desert-*
humans, named *what-does-it-matter-*
if-you-see.

Taken from *Changing Faces*

Bayhead, New Jersey 1906

BETSY SHOLL

No one has thought about destroying the sand dunes.
The young man practicing photography, the grandfather
I have never seen, only focuses on the footprints
spreading across them, and the little boy sliding
down in high buttoned shoes and a white dress.
But he gets the dunes too—in shadow and light
their grasses bent, the sea breaking between peaks.
And the child, rubbing his limbs in wide arcs
to make sand angels, is dwarfed by them—
as though there are places where we know
everything that will happen will happen.

Then, movies are invented and the wind blows
footprints away. Dump trucks, bulldozers
tanks are invented. The sea comes up
to the road in winter. The rich build houses
on stilts, invent *no trespassing* signs.
Newsreels. Depression. Two wars.
Congenital heart disease. The need to know
where we came from. The necessity of proving
the dead used to live, the living
had fathers and mothers.

Taken from *Appalachian Winter*

Bird Watching

BETSY SHOLL

Maybe it's not a lie to say my mother
was once a bird, or two really: one who'd
soar, blue into blue, the other a groundling
endlessly pecking. How she loved binoculars,
loved to reverse *distant* and *close*,

to be off grieving on a high branch
while I tugged at her skirt. What she had to say
about joy could fill an ashtray left out
in the wind, so perhaps it's from her I learned
to tremble on hearing the word *future*,

to worry that the universe can't just expand
forever, and to cringe when the Chinese fortune
says my luck will change. I have to ask
what it is now. Then watching neon rain
splash the restaurant window, those hot pink

mysterious characters flashing off and on,
I wonder if it's all one great unfolding,
impossible to name, so a bird
flying off doesn't have to mean *gone*,
it could mean: look at that bright going.

Taken from *Rough Cradle*

Parsley

MARIE HARRIS

I can't get past the border
the beginning
edges or everything catch
at the corners of my eyelids.
This indecision
is called being only
at the parsley and rue.

She is in need of parsley;
she is dying.

Plain or flat leaved, fern leaved,
moss leaved, Hamburg
or parsnip rooted:
we are all dying alone
and there is so much left
to do together.

Parsley makes a simple green soup.

It is unlucky to transplant parsley
so I am leaving
or
so I am coming home.

Taken from *Raw Honey*

Four Days of Rain

ROBIN BECKER

The sky cracks once and closes.
In the garden, a tiny figure
looks up and hurries away.
The dogs rush in. Someone
runs to shut the windows.
The afternoon goes black.

Dampness like disease is spreading.
For days my socks hang sodden.
Passing from room to room,
I make mental notes—
the roof leaks in the bathroom,
a floorboard is coming up.
I touch a pantsleg; still wet.

Novitiates,
we move about the countryside,
our dark habits
flapping in the wind.

For once all weather reports agree;
no end in sight. *Rain*
I steal an hour out-of-doors
with the mosquitoes to examine
the ground swells, my boots
sinking and sliding in the mud.

I am out in this weather
to recover my faith, to find
a survivor, or a reason
to dance.

Taken from *Personal Effects*

Prairie

ROBIN BECKER

We break off weeds
and put them in each other's mouths.
She slides her fingers
up the milkweed's stem, slits the pod
to watch the seeds float
in the fog beside me.
She pulls me down.
It's the way I thought it would be
when I was seventeen.
The ground is wet. I bury my head
in her chest. She rubs her cheek
against mine—the laws of heat and energy
proven in our bodies.
Here, the illusion of safety—
this is all that matters.
Two women in a field
in the middle of our lives,
while the whole wrecked world
slides into tomorrow.
Her hands come to my body and I would rest
in that simplicity. This field this night
is where we kiss
over and over, clothed, tense.
Before we walk back, she's already walked back,
arranged herself into the familiar fictions.
I remember how she stood among the tourists
the day I thought she wouldn't show,
and we went walking through the galleries
naming the places we'd go: *Etretat,*
Argenteuil, Giverny.

Taken from *Backtalk*

In Conversation

ROBIN BECKER

When your name comes up
in conversation over dinner,
I come to your defense.
She looked beautiful, someone said,
*but unsettled. She left a suitcase
in the shed.* As if you left me here
to cover—an extra ear, hand, eye—
or to mount your reputation.
I know what I know from experience:
you were a strong swimmer;
you defected from your family;
you made love like a person
who had to catch a plane.
By the end of the meal, you're larger
than life, an outlaw with class.
When we gather before the fire,
couples lie in each other's arms,
those alone climb into themselves.
Like a diligent agent
stationed in a foreign country,
I'm waiting for a signal
to come home.

Taken from *Backtalk*

Training the Dog to Come

ROBIN BECKER

is one of the hardest tasks your dog
will have to master. Start early.
Your dog will learn to sit & stay & heel;
perhaps he will read several elementary texts
before he's coming dependably. Do not be discouraged.
If it's summer & you've got one eye
on the raspberry bush, do not expect your dog to be fooled.
If it's fall & you're raking leaves,
your dog will be aware of this shift in your concentration,
& he'll probably take advantage
by taking a train into town.
Various methods may be employed at this juncture:
steak, leg of lamb, but we recommend
that you eliminate food as one incentive;
invest instead in several yards of parachute cord.
While your dog is browsing in the park,
cheerfully call *Come Boomer*
& reel him in. He should come trotting.
Off lead, you're competing with the carcasses of rabbits,
birds dead & alive, dogs just in from other cities
& a host of passionate instincts flickering
in & out of your dog's brain. He will not come.
He probably will not come for some time,
so you should be prepared for this.
In truth, your dog is not much interested in your affairs.
You will have to be more persuasive,
time your calling to coincide with his longing for you—
sporadic, at best, half hearted.

Taken from *Backtalk*

The Conversion of the Jews

ROBIN BECKER

I sat stiffly in the car, resisting
Sunday school & the public school kids
who swore & did it with boys. I went
to a private school during the week,
but in the Sunday school the kids didn't know
anything. Anything. Like when the teacher asked
what the Old Testament was,
I knew it was a source book,
a real history book, but they thought
it was all Jewish miracles.

Their fathers belonged to the Brotherhood
of the Temple & leaned on cars waiting for their kids
to come out with their foul mouths.
Their kids were smoking & touching in the bathroom,
& sometimes the girls peered over the stalls, snickering.
My father bought lox & bagels; it was Sunday &
the table was covered with cream cheese & stinking fish.

On Monday, I'd go to the other school, where
in Religion class, Christ was so handsome & young.
Sure, he had more color, more attraction
than those old guys who, though very smart,
were only making history.
We had Joseph with his coat of many colors
& his brothers & the beautiful Queen Esther.
I'd line up all our guys against theirs,
but somehow Christ, hanging pitiful from that cross—
the nails & spikes sticking into his head—
he always won.

I knew I was on the side of the Old Testament,
but the other kids on my side were so mean
I thought of going over to the New. And it's true
I got a little scared in Debbie Lawson's bedroom:
suspended above her bed, a wooden crucifix
with him hanging & a dime store photo of Mary.
There was no way out of religion

until 6th grade, my friend Annie Post said
Religion was the Opiate of the People.
All those stories, she said—Christ & Moses & Buddha—
everybody had them. Afterwards we had new words
& unshakable beliefs: atheist, agnostic.
Afterwards I felt superior & knew they believed
because they needed to, because they couldn't stand knowing
as Annie & I knew, that it was really accidents
in space, all chemistry & vapors.

Taken from *Backtalk*

Discovery

JEANNINE DOBBS

    Here. See? Here in the clearing—
mushrooms! Edible
sponge,
big floppy ones
like sunhats
    They take me back
to following my Mother's faded gingham
bordered with new rickrack
Me, an acolyte
in middy blouse, Indian belt, cuffed
jeans, scuffed saddles . . .
These, she would say
finding a cache, a colony,
a fairy ring
Our ears would fairly sing with bees, mosquitoes
Over here! I hear her,
see her kneel to fill our woven willow baskets
She and I alone
together inside barbed wire strands
surrounding the last vestiges of virgin land
She showing me how to tell a morel
(dark with a honeycombed cap)
from a toadstool
Wise from the Depression
Mother, thinking mushrooms
something I should know
I thought I could learn nothing new
from her. But then

it was fun
That was thirty years ago
in another state,
but still I know the difference.

See.   These, these are safe.

Taken from *Three Some Poems*

Permission, Berkeley

MARJORIE FLETCHER

I enter behind
the woman who will lecture
and the department chairman.

He says, "I will tell you when . . ."
He says, "If I nod
you ask for questions."

She smiles.
But in angry tornadoes I spin.
She writes their names on the blackboard.

Wharton   Cather   Dickinson

Taken from *33*

Hydrangeas in Early Fall

ELIZABETH KNIES

The bowl of hydrangeas is turbulent as clouds
set on a table; stuck among the clusters

wild phlox and asters, mauve and purple without depth
try to speak. Their efforts are pale and calming.

I put my lips near theirs and hear
a tinted verb in the shape of a petal

while my eyes close upon enormous vistas of pink
and open onto the sea, like balconies.

Taken from *Three Some Poems*

Childbirth

MARILYN ZUCKERMAN

First the waters broke
pouring out of me
like the Flood
For two days I walked
with towels draped
around my thighs
Don't worry the doctor said
you won't remember anything

My grandmother had seven children
Five were born dead
I was too small—and O the pain

When it was my turn
I consulted a magician
A man who smiled and said
Don't worry you won't remember a thing

When it was over
I awoke in a large room
There were flowers
My body was empty
my arms black and blue
from elbows to biceps
See the doctor said *you don't remember . . .*

For weeks after
I dreamed of caves—
and a force like the wind
the ocean screamed

water babies tumbled
in their birth sacs
and no matter how I tried
I couldn't remember anything

Taken from *Personal Effects*

Groundhog

KATHLEEN AGUERO

I could live in a smaller apartment.
I would be happy crowded in one room of books,
walled in by teacups, pillows, fishing gear,
jumbled together.
I would grow fat and still.
Sometimes I think I could live in a hole.

In this large house, I spread my things thin,
and still there are spaces.
I can't have everything I want
at one place
at one time.
I wander from room to room
dragging my favorite possessions.
Always I am rearranging furniture,
trying to shape the perfect corner.
Nothing suits me.

Especially I am afraid of fields.
Large fields.   No mountains to stop them.

Taken from *Thirsty Day*

The Painter

BEATRICE HAWLEY

For the woman's body, use hills,
for the children, use bowls of fruit,
for the house, use lace on a round table.

You paint living in a house,
you are a woman with children who come to visit,
a woman who knows how to use hammer and nails.

For the lovers, paint flowers,
for music, paint the Spanish shawl,
for the mother, paint a bridge.

When the lights go out
and the walls are invisible
the landscapes and still lives
speak to each other about the way
you love them without words;
they tell each other which person they hide.

Taken from *Making the House Fall Down*

The Travel Artist

BEATRICE HAWLEY

Your thinning hair
wreathed in flowers, you
want a white house
near blue water.

Your family, a collection
of rich people, wave you
over oceans to settle
you down to earth.

You write letters to them:
"fire, fire, fire, fire,
my mail is censored the chief
of police is looking this way."

At night you shudder in your
new bed, you spill wine over
the sheets, you pull them
up to your chin.

Taken from *Making the House Fall Down*

Nocturne

BEATRICE HAWLEY

My sisters are writing at the kitchen table.
My father is washing my mother's hair.
I am upstairs looking out the window.
The salt marsh darkens.
I fill my bed with animals.

Taken from *Making the House Fall Down*

Mountains

BEATRICE HAWLEY

Though I stand on mountains
I cannot find my body.
She is washed down by water,
she is missing.
From a long way up
there is no sign,
no red jacket,
no hair making its own rivers.

I have been looking for weeks in these hills.
No one has seen a sign of her.
Not for years on years.
Without my body
I am only light
breaking nothing.

Taken from *Making the House Fall Down*

The Neighbors Celebrate Spring

JOYCE PESEROFF

The neighbors celebrate spring.
A lawnmower ratchets across a lawn,
the cop looks handcuffed to his machine.
Women fly flags of laundry
& dry hair in a prison of pink
rubber rollers.
The smell of burnt flesh pleases
the guest at the barbeque prepared
on a Japanese altar.
The whole neighborhood is praying
to the TV weatherman
some want sun for the beach
some want rain for the peas.
High school girls fornicate rain
or shine or play tennis
in dazzling white sneakers.
At night the men sit out after work
with beers, cigars, gin rummy,
droll stories about trouble
so hard it would break a man
less a man. Then come stories
about fights & after fights,
women. Soon the cigars bloom
like carnations in the dark
& petals of smoke float up to heaven
deceptively crowded with stars.

Taken from *Hardness Scale*

September 7, 1846, *in the desert.*

RUTH WHITMAN

Across the white plain of salt
I see an army of wagons
teams dogs children
passing near the horizon
and rejoice to think
another company
is breaking way for us
heading towards the water

and I see a woman:
long skirted in a bonnet
and beside her another woman
multiplied twenty times
who turns who stops
begins again even as I
turn stop begin
and then I understand

how the need for another being
is turned back on oneself
even as rays of heat
turn back and curve upward
against the reflected image

we discover we are traveling
beside no one
but ourselves

Taken from *Tamsen Donner: A Woman's Journey*

July 25, 1846, *along the Big Sandy*.

RUTH WHITMAN

Thus we scatter as we go along
the arid stretches are so dry
the hills are so steep
that we must constantly tar
and mend the wheels

it would have been better
not to bring
any baggage whatever
only what is necessary
to use on the way

if I were to make this journey again
I would make quite different preparations
    to pack and unpack so many times
    and cross so many streams

the custom of the mountain men
is to possess nothing
and then you will lose nothing

Taken from *Tamsen Donner: A Woman's Journey*

Colors

JANE KENYON

for S.D.

Sometimes I agreed with you
to make you stop telling me things.
I was a fist closed around a rock.

For a long time nothing changed.
It was like driving all day through Texas.

But now I've stopped
tearing the arm off the waiting room chair,
and sneaking back at night to fix it.

And the change was like light
moving through a prism, red
turning to yellow, green to blue,
and all by insensible degrees.

Taken from *From Room to Room*

Six Poems from Anna Akhmatova

JANE KENYON

The memory of sun sickens in my heart,
grass turns yellow,
wind blows the earliest flakes of snow
lightly, lightly.

Already the narrow canals have stopped flowing—
water freezes.
Nothing will ever happen here—
not ever!

The willow against an empty sky makes
a transparent fan.
Maybe it's a good thing I'm not
your wife.

The memory of sun sickens in my heart.
What's this? Darkness?
It's possible! And this may be the first
night of winter.

1911

*

I know, I know the skis
will begin to creak again.
In a dark blue sky a russet moon,
and a sweetly sloping meadow.
The small windows of the palace burn
distant in the stillness.
No track, no path,
only black holes in ice.

Willow, tree of feminine spirits,
don't get in my way.
Shelter the black grackles, black
grackles among your snowy branches.

1913

*

Everything promised him to me:
the fading red rim of heaven,
and a sweet dream on Christmas eve,
and the wind at Easter, ringing,

and the shoots of the red vine,
and waterfalls in the park,
and two large dragonflies
on the rusty iron fencepost.

And I could only believe
that he would be mine
as I walked along the high slopes,
the path of burning stones.

1916

*

Like a white stone in a deep well
one memory lies inside me.
I cannot and will not fight it:
it is joy and it is pain.

It seems to me that anyone who looks closely
into my eyes will notice it immediately,

becoming sadder and more pensive
than someone listening to a melancholy tale.

I remember how the gods turned people
into things, not killing their consciousness.
And now, to keep these glorious sorrows alive,
you have turned into my memory of you.

1916

*

Along the hard crest of the snowdrift
to my white, mysterious house,
both of us quiet now,
keeping silent as we walk.
And sweeter than any song
this dream we now complete—
the trembling of branches we brush against,
the soft ringing of your spurs.

January, 1917

*

A land not mine, still
forever memorable,
the waters of its ocean
chill and fresh.

Sand on the bottom whiter than chalk,
and the air drunk, like wine;
late sun lays bare
the rosy limbs of the pinetrees.

Sunset in the ethereal waves:
I cannot tell if the day
is ending, or the world, or if
the secret of secrets is within me again.

1964

Taken from *From Room to Room*

Here

JANE KENYON

You always belonged here.
You were theirs, certain as a rock.
I'm the one who worries
if I fit in with the furniture
and the landscape.

But I "follow too much
the devices and desires of my own heart."

Already the curves in the road
are familiar to me, and the mountain
in all kinds of light,
treating all people the same.
And when I come over the hill,
I see the house, with its generous
and firm proportions, smoke
rising gaily from the chimney.

I feel my life start up again,
like a cutting when it grows
the first pale and tentative
root hair in a glass of water.

Taken from *From Room to Room*

Finding a Long Gray Hair

JANE KENYON

I scrub the long floorboards
in the kitchen, repeating
the motions of other women
who have lived in this house.
And when I find a long gray hair
floating in the pail,
I feel my life added to theirs.

Taken from *From Room to Room*

The Suitor

JANE KENYON

We lie back to back. Curtains
lift and fall,
like the chest of someone sleeping.
Wind moves the leaves of the box elder;
they show their light undersides,
turning all at once
like a school of fish.
Suddenly I understand that I am happy.
For months this feeling
has been coming closer, stopping
for short visits, like a timid suitor.

Taken from *From Room to Room*

Disclaimer

LEE RUDOLPH

None of these feelings I have are about you.
They are hooks on the ends of long lines,
I stick them into your flesh. The far end
of the line is downstream, in the dark.
There is a hook on that end too,
in the lip of a great blind fish that grows
bigger and bigger every year, blinder and blinder,
wearing itself out swimming against the current
to stay where it is all my life.

Taken from *The Country Changes*

The Fireman's Ball

LEE RUDOLPH

Why did I just buy tickets
to the fireman's ball?
One wants to keep the firemen happy,
definitely one does.—And why
can't poets put on that kind of pressure?
Doesn't the public know the danger
of death by prose—suffocation,
entrapment beneath falling paragraphs?
Do drivers pull cars
to the side of the road
to let the poetry engines by
on their way to put out the doubletalk
at a five-alarm press conference?
Are there jokes about poets' suspenders ("Why
do they wear them?" "To get to the other
side. To make ends meet
meanings. To hold up the world."), does anyone
admire the poets' long brass stanzas,
their black, pliant, waterproof metaphors,
their axes and ladders?
No.

It is time (said the poet) that we organized
a volunteer force, a bucket brigade:
everyone is to have a hand in our survival:
there are arsonists in high places,
and large, careless children
who play with speeches,
and grownups who should know better
who read newspapers in bed
and fall asleep with live lies
burning in their brains,

among us. There should be a poet
in every house, for use in emergencies.
There should be a world
in which we do not have to sell tickets
to the Poets' Ball.

Taken from *The Country Changes*

Dialogue

LEE RUDOLPH

He comes back to us with a story
and won't tell us. He says,
Tell it to me. He passes his hand
over my mouth, and draws out a bird,
a starling. Look, he says, it has a grub
in its beak. And it flies off.—
But he said nothing of the kind,
you tell me; *he said nothing; and he had*
his hands over my *eyes the whole time: he was holding*
my head up from behind.

At night, he serves each one of us
tea, and a tennis ball. He puts one word
into each ear (a fortune in a cookie),
he says: To pay our passage.—*That's not so,*
you say; *it was admission to a play;*
he sat between us, he was holding
(one each) a hand.

When the night was windiest, and the moon full,
he took us to the beach: to overhear
the dialogue. But—*No! that's not clear:*
he was moving his mouth in speech,
but it was the voice of the ocean
inviting us, and I think he knew better
than even whisper: I think he was holding his breath.

Taken from *The Country Changes*

The Old Cemetery

JEFFREY SCHWARTZ

Trees block my way to the grave
but I get there
                  I bring a dog
who disappears behind the old stones
fog horns. no moon
stars are behind clouds
windswept. trees
bend. and climb

I do a dance feeling for
                           stretching
for the horizontal the earth
I can't penetrate
                  the earth
cold
you already are part of

It's under me

under treescarves
and banners
                I go down
to kiss
and smear the dirt
on my face
                to become you
to know you in

your rock
your sleep
your death

Taken from *Contending with the Dark*

The Breadwinner

Man on train: Who is the breadwinner in your family?
Edna: We are all breadwinners.

"You've won the bread!"
I stride toward the platform,
cupping my hands over
the mouths of the cheering audience.
The announcer is concluding,
"and though she doesn't
park worth a damn, she does have a driver's license
and when she shops downtown, the store detectives
don't keep an eye on her . . . ."
but enough of that: I smile,
reaching across him to tear up
his notes, which I don't need any more:
I'm done with trying
to break into sufficiency, counting my efforts,
always detecting new strength.
I take my loaf, brimming with this
adequacy, this
ordinary
grace, laughing it off, posing reluctantly,
making light, talking with my mouth full.

Taken from *Animals*

A History

WILLA SCHNEBERG

She leaves the nursing home
without telling anyone she is going.
She has nothing to do with
the other old women,
discarded by their children too,
who spend their days waiting
from one meal to the next.

Her place is the third chair in
at the long oak table
of Boston Public Library's Reserve Room
where she and her husband spent many evenings,
she reading Janson's HISTORY OF ART,
he reading Will and Ariel Durants'
volumes of civilization.
Before completing the AGE OF NAPOLEON, Volume IV
he died.

Excited as a child waiting for her mother
to whisk sweet cream into whipped,
she opens her spiral notebook
uncaps her ball point pen.

Courbet's SELF PORTRAIT WITH BLACK DOG
shares a page with Millet's THE SOWER.
She thinks of her parents
leaving the wheat fields at sunset in Radomysl.
Weary of making someone else rich,
creeping back to their cottage
to wash themselves in the large tin tub
before preparing supper

of pumpernickel and thick soup
for the children.

When she finds herself in a corridor,
its door locking behind her,
she doesn't call out.
She waits,
listening for the voices of her family
already history.

Taken from *Box Poems*

Misery Loves

L A R K I N   W A R R E N

for B. and B.

You want to bury your dead,
but company is coming.

You open the door. They stand
before you
like carolers.
Their chorus, their litany of names
begins:
grandmother
cousin
wife
lover
child
brother
sister
father.

You carry their list with you,
names plied like coal
in a wooden cart.

You climb into your grief with them,
you are like a miner,
a light on your forehead.
Someone in front holds a canary
to tell you
when you have gone too far.

Taken from *Old Sheets*

Girl

R U T H   L E P S O N

Girl who slides below shadows,
who escapes into rooms at night,
and every morning has time to herself.

The girl with quiet clothes.

A line is broken in her mind.
She bends to collect wood
in the manmade forest.
She is listening intently
for someone to talk to.

Girl with broken shadows,
holding fragments.

Time moves around her like a wind.
There is storm in her voice.
There is no choice in her habits.

Thoughts like small fish
run out of her hands.

Taken from *Dreaming in Color*

The Weather Here

Robert Louthan

for Heather McHugh

When the tough get going, I'm left here alone
in this limited part of the planet.
They write that their new addresses are better,

that I wouldn't think so, and that all is well
with me. O I want to believe them, there's
no sense in relying on first-hand experience

now that I take drugs strong enough to relax
a building. I don't want to look at
the bracelet of scars I started, and boy was I

disappointed that the blood didn't come up blue
like it is under my skin. The weather here
is nice, final. I have some plans, but they're small.

Taken from *Shrunken Planets*

The Birds for Lucie

ANN DARR

My sparrow, my lark, my dove, my
mother, I walk down Pelican Street
and all the birds on your walls
begin to sing. You have made
the singing possible, you
have made the birds rise
until, like an Escher, all
the people I know, meet, love,
fit together form to form to
frame, and the winds begin to
move, the body lifts and
aerodynamics take over.

We are flocking South.

Taken from *Riding with the Fireworks*

Field Exercise

KINERETH GENSLER

You're picking wildflowers in a minefield:

Spread yourself out.
The weight of a body spread-eagled
is safest.
Inch through the dangerous grass
as you would over quicksand.

Such huge anemones! pink,
lavender, the brightest scarlet.
You come through barbed wire,
past signs that say *Keep to the Road*,
This Area Not Cleared of Land Mines.
You could blow yourself up.
You could be arrested.

This is always the border,
this abundance.
You have the whole field to yourself,
as if there were no end to wildflowers
and anyone
could freely fill her arms with flowers.

When picking wildflowers in a minefield,
slide your fingers down each stem.
Snap carefully.
Don't tug at the roots.

Taken from *Without Roof*

For Nelly Sachs

KINERETH GENSLER

Every morning I took a shower
Every morning under the hot spray
tuned by my hand
I saw the valves
streaming gas
from the walls and ceilings
of rooms marked "BATH"
in Buchenwald   Bergen-Belsen

As if I'd been there
As if it were required of me
As if all Jews
were forced to start each day
stripped in a locked room
remembering in their skins
unable to stop it
just as one by one women
like me had stood
packed in a locked room
under the streaming gas
unable to stop it

Give us this day
the grace
of showers

I can't remember when it stopped
In the crush of body-counts
in the years of drought & floods
& saturation bombing
I lost them all

they went up
in numbers

O the showers Nelly
the showers
where I stand alone   graceless

This numbness
like the end of all desire
the terrible forgetting in my body

Taken from *Three Some Poems*

Destination

KINERETH GENSLER

I arrive at the animals reluctant
to use them
we ourselves should be enough
the stories are about us
as for birds they've always stood for
the unknowable verbs
as for grass grain flowers that shake the earth
with small unstoppable explosions
as for bonsai trees and redwoods
the extremes of butterfly and rock
as for grasshopper and ant
grapes and the fox
all Aesop's fables
those creatures that stand for us
stand also for themselves
as you and I stand also for ourselves
nobody's animals

Taken from *Without Roof*

Freshman, 1939

KINERETH GENSLER

She lived in the dorm with us,
a loud-mouthed rich girl whose daddy
was terra cotta king of the U.S.A.
We, too, came from someplace:
downstate Illinois, Chicago, Hawaii.
I came from Jerusalem.
She'd been to boarding school in Munich,
had a boyfriend in the German Air Force.
At the fraternity ball,
dressed as a popular song,
"I'm Stepping Out with a Memory Tonight,"
she wore a full-dress Nazi Luftwaffe uniform.

Such bad taste,
said the girls of Kelly Hall.
So horrid for her date.

In crowded bull sessions in the dormitory,
her subject was Jews:
how she could smell them in any crowd.
It was a sense one could develop.
Daddy's friend Goebbels had it.
Any Jews in this room?—
No, she said, checking us out.
The three Jews, with their bland faces
and unobtrusive pores, did not speak up.
By the time we graduated,
it made no difference.
In Munich, the ones like us had been identified.

Taken from *Journey Fruit*

Lowell Reading

JOHN HILDEBIDLE

Everyone seems to know him,
to expect a nod of recognition
on his way up to the podium,
stooped, oddly diffident;
that heavy rusted thing reputation
hangs on him like an old suit
too well-worn to throw out.

He reads "Lepke" and a poem to Berryman
and "My Last Afternoon with Uncle Devereux"
and stops to identify each cousin.
The crowd acts as if it's no news to them.
Even when the words on the page
hold no possible laughter, he laughs,
interrupting in mid-sentence to explain the joke
in a voice almost Southern, softened
perhaps by Ireland, perhaps by living or practice,
a voice so unlikely to surprise.

The dark varnished wood of the stage
has in the dim light the glow
of old museum cases, as he looms there
like a naturalist not quite used to lecturing,
this tall, bent, aging, gentle man
who holds his battered mind at arm's length
to puzzle its peculiar anguish into speech,
and smiles as if there is something
absolute and calming he would tell us all
if we didn't know so much, if
the accident of words could bear the weight.

Taken from *The Old Chore*

Wait

SUSAN SNIVELY

—*sign above Kafka's desk*
(for Robert Hahn)

Good whiskey, neat, can break
the ice. At the bottom of the glass
there are words you must get to, but
they can wait. You lean back,
resting your head full of syllables.

Faces of people you have loved
swim toward you briefly
then retreat, older suddenly
in the approaching shade.

Nothing to do now
except obey the singular law
of the poet's lawless life:
to love people,
to see them go

and then to go inside, while the evening
still looks like the afternoon,
before it is too late,
and begin:
shutting a door to the rest of the house

thinking of the books to be accomplished
and the poems in them, unavoidable now,
factual as children
who speak the truth.

Taken from *The Distance*

Dust

SUSAN SNIVELY

When they opened me there was a smell of flowers—
delphinia, olive leaves, berries of nightshade
which crumbled like skin, giving off fragrance
as the centuries leaped into the air.
My flesh had joined my bones,
rotted by dried unguents, stuffed with linen.
I have become my own buried kingdom.

The boat never comes, the bird flies away
into the sun, and the sun disappears
under a lid of gold and glass. Long since
I have put aside my gifts: the slings and bows,
the diadem, the chariot of wine. In eternity
you hear the sound of water like an endless song
sung by your mother before you were conceived.

If you become a temple, you will be an eternal mystery,
dark eyes under a cloak of stone,
moving through history like a heavy ghost.
What was my life? On a painted chest
my queen is stroking my shoulder with balm.
In an alabaster jar
lies the burnt remnant of my heart.

They went back through the long tunnels, leaving prayer
to seal my dead city. Under the wind and sun
the sand heaves silently. O God, I am but a little space,
a nest of dead wings. . . .
You who open my soul, remember me in my youth,
even as I was on the day I was born,
hastening toward death on golden feet.

Taken from *The Distance*

Come a Daisy

JACQUELINE FRANK

That the spirit should hold is rare:
such troubles we have seen!
Fire consumes beyond itself to die
before we know it has been.
Meanwhile, the seasons proceed,
defeat anger. Nature is wise,
or its indifference may mean
there is little upon which to rely.

Yet small daisies carry our weight.
A stubborn lark, raindrops, a smell:
we are undone, we cry for help!
Come a daisy, I shall be there!
Let the fire grow into its height.
That the spirit should hold is rare.

Taken from *No One Took a Country from Me*

Passing Through Les Eyzies

JACQUELINE FRANK

The swallows on the telephone wire
give up to the rain that rises
until they tremble within their wings.
They wait as only waiting can be,
for nothing but that it should cease.

The nun's fingertips tell her beads.
Her knuckles keep their own time,
but her body gives up to the train's lashings.
Her lids open, close, open, and her eyes,
what do her eyes see that look nowhere?

Not to the stationmaster's wife
who stares, her arms akimbo as we pass,
her linen dripping on the line;
or the stationmaster who waves his flag,
the caves gaping above him.

Not Cro-Magnon. The sun never touches
his stone entrances that climb through fern
and brambles down to the river.
Only the river can relieve us from Cro-Magnon,
from his children born like beads.

The river leads somewhere else.
"Give up!" say the swallows, the nun's fingertips,
the holes in the rock, the stationmaster's flag.
"Give up! You have come home as far
as you may ever come, go back to, or remain."

Taken from *No One Took a Country from Me*

Argument for Parting

Miriam Goodman

Remember your list of bottles from the dump?
I think of how you find a way to quantify—
list the miles you skated,
the towns where we made love.
If things add up, you can be happy.
You cut wood daily and the pile accumulates.
Your days become a history.

By all means of dailiness, the over-all
is done. Who will know I broke my daughter's
will or poured the alphabet into her ear?
Who else will know I loved you?
Oh sad arithmetic, my name amounts to nothing.
Would you number it on lists? There were
no witnesses; I improvised.

And I don't marry.
I don't buy land.
I get older by myself.

Taken from *Signal::Noise*

The Birdcarver

DAVID McKAIN

Wanting us to see more than decoys
he talks with a knife about his dream:
to free the birds that nest inside the mind,
carve them out of words until they soar.

The white cedar's nearly gone, he says,
sold for posts and fences—
that's the wood for the long-beaked shore birds,
for their hull, nothing else will do.
For fan-tail, ring-neck or mallard,
the soft white pine from Utah.

But the neck of the shore bird curves,
turns to head, then swerves
into a beak
from an everyday branch of blueberry—

that's the thing of it,
find the right day, be ready to see,
come up on it eye-level,
the exact right stem, one
you've passed a hundred times
now curlew, Hudsonian, heron.

The native white cedar,
cut it winter from the swamp,
drag it on a sled across the ice
to season a year up on stickers—
that's a big part, getting out.

Then know calls, migrations, the moon—
like anybody with wood and time,
making something out of nothing.

Taken from *The Common Life*

40 Nights on a River Barge

C ATHERINE   A NDERSON

for my brother Bill

Six hours on and six hours off,
and before your last shift of sleep,
the Ohio river could easily turn itself back
until the slow shoulders working alongside you
become the banked hills of Indiana,
two long brown slopes on either side
and a wood freckling downstream.
This is your final haul home,
switchback over the skin of an aging country.
The Union Army once buried their prisoners
sitting upright here in the shallow banks,
one head touching another, bending leeward.
All spring they seem to sweat with you
into the water,
as if the rain settling around your neck
could never be as lasting as their breath.

Taken from *In the Mother Tongue*

Lettuce

ERICA FUNKHOUSER

In June, the new lettuce
appears in tidy rows
with the logic of impulse.
The curly heads sit
as if they had landed
during the night
from some outer nebula,
their mere existence genius,
whatever brought them here
irrelevant.

As if a single curve
experienced a single time
were too delicate
even to be eaten,
each head repeats itself
from leaf to leaf.

The inner leaves
are smaller, stiffer,
and the inmost leaves,
receiving the least light,
are all succulence,
their tiny curves
curled around a milky stalk.

Taken from *Natural Affinities*

Translating Tsvetayeva

CELIA GILBERT

I speak with her hoarse sorrow,
my voice extinguished
as I bring hers back
from long silence.

I could disappear, pulled
into her orbit. Or crack,
like clay unequal
to her fire.

Afterwards, empty, I'm lost.
The simplest things look strange,
unclear. Reaching for you, I begin
to spell out my old life again.

And yet, she knows, even though you
hold me in your arms,
I'll return to her: those eyes
that tried to outstare the sun,
the mouth that *tasted the night*.

Taken from *Bonfire*

Through Glass

CELIA GILBERT

The sun, a pale insomniac, struggles
through frosted panes of kitchen glass.
What had he said, innocent ten-year-old,
that made my sobs begin? My mouth sags.
He's looking down at me bent over the sink
in my old green bathrobe.
I know I should stop; I feel his panic. "Stop!" he says.
"You might go crazy."
He said, that first night when I came to put him to bed,
"This is too terrible. We mustn't think about it any more."
He looks too much like the sister he loved.
Will we ever talk?
"Make sure you eat," he says, picking up his school bag.

Taken from *An Ark of Sorts*

The Promise

Suzanne E. Berger

For those afraid of the dark
and its empty sleeves,
there is a place lit by animal-comfort—
to hold against the skin,
fur to the naked pelt of ourselves

Listen, whole families speak there,
the geodes of their words, glowing:
There will be waking,
there will be enough bread

And taste the rain there:
It harvests a repair people dream of
Its crops shine with the after-taste
of sun and morning

Enter, look closely, lean towards
this far place,
somewhere its bright seeds scattered
in the planet of the body

Taken from *Legacies*

Steptoe Butte

SUE STANDING

The man we asked for directions
had a hand the shape of a peony,
one blossom in dry country.

We're travelling light—
that stubble, this river,
too many bandages in common.

From this height
my field glasses contain
blank and white

acres of ruined wheat.
It's someone else's land
sculpted around moraines,

quilted with soil. Clouds
form an aperture above us—
a cloudless lens.

There's too much and too little.
We call the wind a fossil,
try photographing all of it.

Taken from *Deception Pass*

Kansas, Sunstruck

JOAN JOFFE HALL

His truck parked at roadside
in late afternoon, the man stares
across the cornfield at a foam of clouds.
The door opens and a child
steps down. She is around eight, blind,
puts her hand on the fender
for balance. Shadows of clouds
race sunshine through the corn.
"Cloud," she says, and "sun."
They practice this game
as if her father made the weather.
When it holds, sunstruck
she presses her other hand
on the metal to gather warmth
and turns her face toward the sun,
ready to fly away. The man
watches like a murre about to plunge
with its chick in first flight
from a cliff overlooking the sea.

Taken from *Romance & Capitalism at the Movies*

from Mission Hill

FANNY HOWE

Proximity of prayer
is like a little well's
way into the beautiful

black. Here, words drill
a path for a sailing soul — if —

the sky has ears

Writing with stars
the spirit dabbles
where endings never are

But somewhere a donkey's warm
chewing on grass

It's where,
sweet earth, the soul aspires, back

Taken from *Robeson Street*

The Nursery

FANNY HOWE

The baby
         was made in a cell
in the silver & rose underworld.
Invisibly imprisoned
               in vessels & cords, no gold
for a baby; instead
eyes, and a sudden soul, twelve weeks
old, which widened its will.

      *

Tucked in the notch of my fossil: bones
        laddered a spine from a cave,
the knees & skull
were etched in this cell, no stone, no gold
where no sun brushed its air.

      *

One in one, we slept together
    all sculpture
           of two figures welded.
But the infant's fingers
squeezed & kneaded
           me, as if to show
the Lord won't crush what moves
on its own . . . secretly.

      *

On Robeson Street
                       anonymous
was best, where babies
have small hearts
                to learn
with;
        like intimate
thoughts on sea
water, they're limited.

           *

Soldered to my self
   it might be a soldier or a thief
for all I know.
The line between revolution & crime
   is all in the mind
      where ideas or righteousness
and rights confuse.

           *

I walked the nursery floor.
By four-eyed buttons & the curdle of a cradle's
paint: a trellis of old gold
   roses, lipped & caked
where feet will be kicking in wool.

           *

      Then the running,
the race after,
cleaning the streets, up for a life.
His technicolor cord
hung from a gallery of bones,

but breathing, *I'm finished.*
Both of us.

*

And when the baby sighed,
through his circle of lips,
                    I kissed it,
          and so did he, my circle to his,
we kissed ourselves and each other,
          as if each cell was a Cupid,
          and we were born in it.

*

The cornerstone's dust
up-floating

by trucks & tanks.
White flowers spackle

the sky crossing the sea.
A plane above the patio

wakes the silence
and my infant who raises

his arms to see
what he's made of.

O animation! O liberty!

Taken from *Robeson Street*

The Hunt

HELENA MINTON

I touch the pelt nailed to the wall,
black tail, black stripe along the spine.
I want to pull it over my shoulders
and walk out, bare feet burning
on the icy streets.

                    After you shot the buck
you had to shoo away three deer,
which sat beside it.
Wind blew toward your face.
You left the head in the moss,
eyes black and glassy.

Last night I went back for the skull,
picked clean in tundra snow.
It spoke but soil absorbed its words.
What I held was your head,
hollowed in tundra air.
I knew I would leave my body
next to yours.

                Turning in sleep
I saw the deer stand up again,
sheathed in sunlight as you shouted.
Lifting their heads in the wind
they blinked, their eyes not quite believing.

Taken from *The Canal Bed*

Dream

CAROLE OLES

I am delivered to Harvard
in a black carriage with curtains

The lecture hall churns
men lining the walls, leaning
over balconies

I approach the podium

They continue their conversations

I open my mouth to begin
and my teeth spill out
powdery as chalk

A man in the front row
rushes onstage to gather them

I ask are there questions

and he writes with my tooth
on the blackboard

How do you eat enough to stay alive?

Taken from *Night Watches: Inventions on the Life of Maria Mitchell*

Migrations

ALLISON FUNK

Canada geese over bone-white fields:
in autumn the constellation
moved above the house and disappeared.
I watched from the broken corn,
empty as the sky after the birds' departure.

It seemed longer than a season
that I counted the dead husks.
If you lose a child, they say,
there is no comfort
until you hear the unborn
call again for direction.

When the birds come back
it is never in clouds or arrows.
One small burden of proof,
a sparrow appears on the lawn.
Then gradually as a five-month baby
unfurls and tries the drum,
thrush, warbler, robin
and swallow congregate and sing.

Winter is still the longest season.
When the branch starts to bend
we cannot return to the warm continent
we traveled from.
But there are moments when it is enough
that my son journeyed at night and arrived.

Taken from *A Form of Conversion*

Crosscut and Chainsaw

L I N N E A   J O H N S O N

The crosscut handsaw is mine; I have brought it
from the chew of birch, the swift felling of willow,
the hot ache of an old oak dead two winters
outside my city windows, crying for the blade to lay it
     down.

Yours would as soon tear through my limbs
as the wood we walk to find, could cut the tires off your
     pickup
at fifty miles an hour, howls through air
eating its own screams to increase velocity.

I am in love with you from the neck down
looking for firewood from a finished orchard:
its seasoning will outlast our own. Today,

the give of leaf loam, the sky blue enough to die from,
the blaze of these Fall woods link us one hand each,

the other of our hands to our saws. I do not know
how you love me but I do know you are wrong
about the wood and how to cut it.

Taken from *The Chicago Home*

Black Dog

MARGO LOCKWOOD

I see my children learn
to lean away from me,
avoiding my anger with a grin
the wrong size.

And why not, I say,
who raised them up alone,
hoping that the wind
would temper to the shorn lambs?

Not in ways that would have them
grow too gentle though –
so that in their adulthood
there would be nothing common
to us all.

I see too many
soft in the wrong place
who flinch and yield
at every prod
who bury their face
in their hands
too often –

so that the gesture
loses its terrible purity.

Taken from *Black Dog*

The Hermit

TOM ABSHER

It is strange to say it,
but I have turned out to be someone
who likes no one else.
Like you I have spent my life with people,
but all those years I was most lonely for myself.
That woman I looked for everywhere
is inside my own laughter. I keep a small bed—
the body is not what I want either.

One after another my doors close softly
with the word no. In the back room
I watch the snow falling out of the sky
making everything the same color.
Winter and I have a talent for emptiness—
this is going to be a sweet exile.

Taken from *The Calling*

Fish

TOM ABSHER

It's my night for dishes
so everyone has left the kitchen.
There on the cutting board
the head of a brook trout
we had for supper. A *brookie*
to the kids who caught it.
I look at the face, the dour fish face
with its flat eye. At the table
we talked about eating animals.
The children won't eat venison—
Deer are spiritual, they say.
Trout are a dime a dozen.

I know what they mean,
but while I ate I kept thinking
about the fish, its lifetime in the lake,
how it travelled all day
through layers of color
down into shadowed zones of boulders
and sunken logs. About
its being drawn to sunlight
polishing the water's surface, brilliant,
a fish's heaven.
Holding its body perfectly still
in a cold current feeding the lake,
watching with those eyes which never close,
how like a god it must have felt
in that sliver of flesh
which was its heart.

Taken from *The Calling*

Omen
CAROLE BORGES

Pinks and reds...
a woman stands on a porch
watching tulips drink rainwater.
When they've taken too much
they fall down.

The woman is thinking
about nothing, wisps of thought,
images that change and alter.
She stands with her hands on a railing,
her body stiff as a pillar of wood.
Inside her red shirt her breasts
float up and down.
She knows if she moves too quick
this moment will collapse.

From an upstairs window
her husband watches her.

She knows he watches, but
she's not willing to
wave her hand or smile.

Something's moving beneath the porch.
She doesn't know what,
but it's wild.

Taken from *Disciplining the Devil's Country*

The Doors
NINA NYHART

At certain times the inner elevator goes down
    and finds a woman so passionate
    she can't live outside a human body.
And then the starlings all take off as one
    and she begins to rise.

Up and down, up and down—she's not that simple.

Sometimes she carries a basket—
    old-fashioned wicker, a looped handle,
    filled with flames.
Or, she lies in bed after giving birth,
    her baby too close to the edge.
    Is she irresponsible?

She wants to swim in the river that flows uphill.

The doors—soft, powerful,
    open and close like sea anemones—
    scarlet, pink, silver,
and there is the urge to dive deeper,
    to listen more closely…

Taken from *French for Soldiers*

Ink Blots

LAUREL TRIVELPIECE

Try hard to think hard,
flat. And the smooth
field in front of you
swells from its moorings,
the mind being first
among all tethered things

Or why these cattle?
Standing, doubled by shadows,
in this stream?
Fragments of what might be
an orderly complicity tend
to blow like ink blots in the wind

To measure the darkness before you,
and the dust after,
your father came,
nightly was crossed
by the moon's white action,
his journey drying under his shoes

Passing through — as if there would
be a time when the leaves and the hours
and the questions fall away and
you are no longer separate
from the mute business of stone,
the workings of water

The answer you no longer need
tapers off into a shadow,
simply fallen,
and flickering with the stream

Taken from *Blue Holes*

Evening Calm

FORREST GANDER

After the strangling of each first son
an overture of sighs
floated the streets.
You think of this
watching fog.
It lifts off the lake
like a soldier getting up
from a foreign war. He halts
on your land for a drink. Water
clouds over and churns in your well.

Outside hundreds stumble by.
They are not injured. You,
not dreaming. Another drifts
down your path who does not want water.

The moon depends from the earth
like an ear. While the cold

ferrets into your lungs,
boots crack the garden's hard pan.
These are the ones past thirst
trained by strangers with latches

softly clicking in their voices.
In the pitch they see
every detail. They've come

to return something. Not their gear.
Their hands clench and open like flowers.
When you approach the garden
ruby-throated birds fly.

Taken from *Rush to the Lake*

Particles

NORA MITCHELL

After I leave her I lie down on her lawn
and wonder what to do next.
Stretched out, I stare at the sky.
In all that daylight
I feel dark inside and close my eyes.
Through my shirt I feel the dirt,
the small stones and roots.
My breath moves the length of my body.
It reaches the base of my spine and warms my gut.
I am clean, I let it clean me out.
My vertebrae nestle into the grass
like a flock of sparrows
disappearing into a field.
My palms and fingers go flat and still.
I imagine her at one of the windows above me,
lifting a curtain, staring down,
and seeing nothing.
At night the lights from her house
will tumble out onto the lawn
in rectangular patches,
until, one by one, she extinguishes the lamps,
leaving a single bulb high up.
That will be her, burning in sleep.

Taken from *Your Skin Is A Country*

My World

H E L E N E D A V I S

I know the dizzying path from my bed to the bathroom, the
icy feel of the sink under my fingers, my chin. The smell of
the bath oils and powders on the shelf. I know exactly how
many minutes it will take Martha to run down the hill to my
house when I call her for help. I know by heart the stained-
glass colors of my night light that I leave on every night
although I can now find my way through the house blind. I
know the hard, white edges of my wicker chair where I first
felt my hair prickle and then die. I know that outside,
mysteriously, people are always finding something to
celebrate. Thanksgiving, Christmas, New Year's. Lights, gift
wraps. The crinkle of ribbons. A friend gets married.
Another has a baby.

Here, in my world, I know only the silk of my cat against my
skin, always there in my bed, always there when I'm ill. I
breathe a cat's breath, rumble in my chest—a purr. I want to
slink into a cat's sleep, leave my body for awhile, the smell of
medicine in my body, my rooms, the white foam I vomit. But
every time I look, it's midnight. I take my "rescue" pill. I sit
in the wicker chair. I expect to hear the sound of the devil
clanging through the hallway outside my door.

Taken from *Chemo-Poet and Other Poems*

Windfall

NANCY DONEGAN

In Santa Ana
unabating wind for days,
a diet of dust.
The warehouse door unlatched.
Three-thousand straw sombreros
funnel into the sky.
They are swooped up
like hollow birds.

A few flop over,
caught in a cross current.
Hot air is sucked
into their bowls,
they droop, earthbound
dry old mouths.

A woman in Magdalena
sees them fall.
She scrambles to the high plateau,
stretches her body up full.
She is dwarfed by the saguaro,
her torn apron blows over her head,
but she is shouting now,
crazy for a yellow hat.
The ribbons she forgot
for twenty years
are streaming down her back.

Taken from *Forked Rivers*

The Rain

SABRA LOOMIS

When I awoke, it was in sunlight.
Soft words were spoken nearby; in the distance
a schoolbell chimed. I had such messages!
I wanted to roll out over hillsides,
speak into rivers . . .

To have walked over the wide earth,
a pilgrim, knocking softly at your door,
kneeling at the thresholds. Waking,
to descend into twilight . . .

O Sister, I cannot tell you enough
in this one time of falling,

this hurrying forest,
the wakeful silence that is myself.

Taken from *Rosetree*

December Coming In

ROSAMOND ROSENMEIER

You are knocking with a great knock,
and I am running down the long stairs all the way
to open the front door, unlatched,
pulled—like that—wide to you:
firm standing, pleased with yourself, where twined
on each post of the lintel the euonymous climbs over,
evergreen stems almost trees, hanging
with red berries in this season.

The sun behind you blinds me while I stand believing
you have pulled off your gloves
and stepped over the threshold.
All the sun thrusts in with you,
flooding the fire's hearth, the walls,
the hall floor shining, until,
like chandeliers, all my candles burn,
and the wine is poured, is poured.

Taken from *Lines Out*

Mandelstam

JEAN VALENTINE

> *1934-35. The time of his arrest and imprisonment in Moscow, and
> his exile, with his wife Nadezhda Jakolevna Khazina, to Voronezh.*

My mother's house
Russia
Calm are the wolf's bronze udders,
calm the light around her
fur, out-starred with frost

I am 43
Moscow we will not live

Russia
Iron shoe
its little
incurved length and width

Russia   old
root cellar   old mouth of
blood under-the-earth
pulling us down into herself
no room to lie down

    and your poor hand
    over and over
    draws my brain
    back to your breast's small
    campfire

Voronezh we won't live
    not even my hand
    to hold your hand, useless.

Taken from *Home. Deep. Blue*

The River at Wolf

JEAN VALENTINE

Coming east we left the animals
pelican beaver osprey muskrat and snake
their hair and skin and feathers
their eyes in the dark: red and green.
Your finger drawing my mouth.

Blessed are they who remember
that what they now have they once longed for.

A day a year ago last summer
God filled me with himself, like gold, inside,
deeper inside than marrow.

This close to God this close to you:
walking into the river at Wolf with
the animals. The snake's
green skin, lit from inside. Our second life.

Taken from *The River at Wolf*

To Plath, to Sexton

JEAN VALENTINE

So what use was poetry
to a white empty house?

Wolf, swan, hare,
in by the fire.

And when your tree
crashed through your house,

what use then
was all your power?

It was the use of you.
It was the flower.

Taken from *The River at Wolf*

A Hum To Say I'm Missing Your Touch

Carol Potter

to Paula

Water breaking from rocks. Finally
a sound to undo the drum of crickets
pushing summer to its limit.
This green slide on my skin, this sound
I straddle, water on water
on rocks filled with light like the light
inside me when you un-buckle my limbs with your
lips breathing air into me until I float
in your hands the way I float now down
this river, swimming, you singing your way
into me, swimming, singing, making my body
outgrow its house of bone, its breath of air,
its hard tales it likes to tell.
This sound finally larger than the sound
of trucks passing by the river, larger
than the voices of children playing
at the water's edge, larger than the patience
of mothers watching those children play, as large
as the hum you set thrumming when you tongue this
nest of hair making my skin swell from the wet V
of my thighs held here now above the water
slipping through rocks singing this thrum,
this hum remembered in your name.

Taken from *Before We Were Born*

Night Dive

JEFFREY GREENE

The seabeds are nocturnal.
Even on the searocks in the shallows
green crabs cling in starlight.

Boys pull on their neoprene suits
and arrive in the black ocean
looking down for lobsters.

The sealife slows under their lanterns.
In the same way the moon
would jacklight us on the bare shore.

In your right hand you can hold a lantern,
and with your left hand
you can touch the blind fish.

This is the element you love so well,
your body without light
in the ocean without light.

Tonight, Mother, I could lose you
as you sleep under the clear surface
of an oxygen tent.

I have come back to New England,
to this house where now there is no one.
I turn on lights and the rooms go on sleeping.

This is the night dive
where the slow halibut lifts like a table,
where the eel swims from a bed of skins,

and where the lobster
goes forward with its one crushing claw
and its one tearing claw.

Taken from *To the Left of the Worshiper*

The Choice

NANCY LAGOMARSINO

Her circumstance is so different from mine, she doesn't want
a child right now. She would rather die than bring another
child with its sand pail into this world.

I don't want her child either — my own children are
oceans that surround me. To deny her is to refuse help to one
who has drunk poison.

What of the unborn child?

Don't think of it as a child. If there's no other choice, think
of it as a dream the body had.

Taken from *The Secretary Parables*

Remission

PAMELA STEWART

In the tall russet-flecked trees of autumn
some bird coughs repeatedly. The thunk
of an ax from a distant hill
sends rooks screeching like warning. Slowly,
a man walks with that cadence
which lifts one foot, then the other,
to punctuate present from past.
What he's not, who he's not, clicks
into this figure on a path
which will return to the exact door
closed just minutes ago.

In this damp air, the thin skin of his wrists
shines. Breeze slicks through his hair.
Before long his bones will break
their disguise and drift out to sea.
His blood knows this, knows how first
he learned to hide away the feathers, pebbles,
and treasured words of childhood
in pockets and drawers. Then he learned
to hide himself. Now all we see
is someone in a forest scuffing leaves
against freshening wind.

Taken from *Infrequent Mysteries*

Painting

ALICE JONES

He'd go down to the basement
wearing his dark blue work shirt,
to the corner of the windowless,
cinder-block room where he had
his canvas propped, and somehow,
after years of being tangled up
in knots of possibility, after
days of talk, after wrestling
with the angel of Not-painting,
he squeezed a wildly orange
Vermont landscape out of those
bright oily tubes, smeared it,
all its red-leafed, golden blur,
onto the rectangle of cloth
and gesso that had been waiting,
like me, for his stroking hand.

Taken from *The Knot*

His Body Like Christ Passed In And Out Of My Life

TIMOTHY LIU

A woman selling Bibles at the Greyhound station.
Me waiting. I was not indifferent, only hardened.
A German violin instead of her voice. Headphones
in my ears. The smell of that place, diesel and Brahms.
Me waiting as others wait. Me turning the cassette,
she turning pages in that purgatory without deliverance.
Later my lover smiling as Jesus, always late, never
his fault. Me looking back at a woman praising God.
Her devotion. My envy. A desire for permanence.
For a world without betrayal. I think of that winter,
the tracks outside my window erased from a field
of snow, me ironing sheets as if no one had slept
there. A bus heading South without me. My car
not starting, dead batteries, an empty walkman
discarded under the bed. How the world slides away.
Me diminished by the thought of him. Of spring.
What are birds returning, singing, compared to this,
the lives that I have forsaken to honor a god.

Taken from *Vox Angelica*

Equinox: The Goldfinch

Cheryl Savageau

it is as if he had swallowed the sun
which slept the winter inside him
until he forgot what it was like
to live in warmth, and golden.
but his body has the knack of timing.
for weeks now golden feathers
have appeared among the grey and khaki brown
now his back is mottled with ice floes
drifting in water that is not blue
but shining the purest yellow

he rides upon the cusp of winter
and he is full of sun
it is too much for him to bear
his throat swells with it
and he pushes the sun out
into the air where it turns
immediately to song. The notes

fall back to him, and he tries again,
head back, throwing the sun
into the air, and it returns
to him, and yet again,
and again, there is no end
to this light that is filling him,
it is the sun he has become the sun.
his song shimmers with light
and his body blossoms
into yellow

Taken from *Home Country*

Comes Down Like Milk

CHERYL SAVAGEAU

My mother's curls
have come undone.
She washes her mother's legs
and covers them
in clean sheets.
When we lean over
to turn her shrunken body
Memere takes a sharp breath.
My mother and I become still,
our bodies grow bigger
trying to absorb the pain.

We wait for the soft moan.
Instead, Memere grasps
the braid running down my back.

While I adjust the pillow,
my mother gets comb and brush.
Together we take out the pins.
Memere's hair comes down like milk.

Taken from *Home Country*

Coming Down Rain From Light

Margaret Lloyd

My friend tells me she does not know
why she has a body anymore

and of course she is talking about
not being loved. I don't know what to say

but think of two poems
my daughter wrote last month.

One called "Coming Down Rain from Light"
about our roof leaking through a light socket.

The other, she said, was private
and I had to go into the next room

to hear her poem about rejection.
Even at four she has learned to hide

how she does not feel loved.
I think of a day years ago

when I sat in a seminar
smelling of semen, enjoying

the display that allows
people to imagine

I have been touched, my voice
heard, my body entered,

that perhaps I am loved
but at the least, I have been desired.

I love my children,
I hug them. In the dark

I put my mouth
on the neck of a man I love.

I don't care if God passionately pursues me.
If I have a body, I want another body.

Sweat, semen, the juices of our mouths
are rain from light

and I can find no words of comfort
for my friend today.

Taken from *This Particular Earthly Scene*

Father's Day

SUZANNE MATSON

The day feels difficult, vagrant,
hot from the start, even in the park at 10 a.m. when I come holding
my paper cup of coffee. No one would say the day
wasn't beautiful; no one would say it wasn't drenched in green
underwater light.

One father, mine, sits far away and waits to die, mumbling
old grudges to his tireless self. After
the attendants have given up on his eyeglasses,
dentures, and shave, after he has batted
them all away in a rage, he sits

pissed off and bony, a gray silt of whiskers
and wild brows and flaking skin. He wanted to hit
his only granddaughter, brought blinking to him in flannel
at three months. But let us not dwell
on that. Let us dwell on the rhythmic ringing notes

of his hammer in the backyard thirty years ago,
when my father frowned in concentration
over the framing of a small house soon to be
shingled and roofed and painted the exact same shade
as the house we lived in in real life.

The small house was my brother's first house
of his own. I was a baby in a bonnet.
My brother and father conferred in serious tones
over the placement of the door. And everything was green:
the big house, the little house, the backyard and our tightly
    furled lives.

Taken from *Durable Goods*

Available Light

DAVID WILLIAMS

When I think of how you bled to death
during the siege of Beirut,
your face dissolves into grains of silver
bromide, rocks on the moon
we see as a human face.

*

There was a girl who spent the winter in bed
because she was hungry and had no shoes.
Her father painted flowers for her
on the wall. A man took her picture there
in the Warsaw Ghetto. Her image survives.

*

I pick you out among all the lost,
a Jew, an Arab, who both could have passed
for my daughters, your trace dark crystals
on a negative, breath on a mirror,
a steady, invisible light.

*The central section refers to a photograph
by Roman Vishniac.*

Taken from *Traveling Mercies*

Bamboo Bridge

DOUG ANDERSON

We cross the bridge, quietly.
The bathing girl does not see us
till we've stopped and gaped like fools.
There are no catcalls, whoops,
none of the things that soldiers do;
the most stupid of us is silent, rapt.
She might be fourteen or twenty,
sunk thigh deep in green water,
her woman's pelt a glistening corkscrew,
a wonder, a wonder she is; I forgot.
For a moment we all hold the same thought,
that there is a life in life and war is shit.
For a song we'd all go to the mountains,
eat pineapples, drink goat's milk,
find a girl like this, who cares
her teeth are stained with betel nut,
her hands as hard as feet.
If I can live another month it's over,
and so we think a single thought,
a bell's resonance.
And then she turns and sees us there,
sinks in the water, eyes full of hate;
the trance broken.
We move into the village on the other side.

Taken from *The Moon Reflected Fire*

Short Timer

DOUG ANDERSON

Twelve hours before his plane was to lift off for home
he was sitting in the EM club
slugging down Filipino beer.
A sniper round rang through the tin roof,
knocked him off his stool, a near complete flip
before he hit the floor.
Next thing I knew we were lugging him
through the sand toward the sick bay;
him bucking and screaming,
me trying to shield the spurting head,
the sniper bearing down on us,
the others scattering to the perimeter to return fire.
Inside we saw how bad it was.
I syringed the long gash in the parietal with sterile water,
the doctor with a flashlight looking close,
the man saying, *Oh God,* and already the slur,
the drool. He would live. Go home.
Sit the rest of his life in front of a television set.
Back in the EM club they had wiped up the blood
and we could see the stars
through the thirty caliber holes in the roof.
What was in the 20 cc's of brain he lost?
These are things that can occupy a drunk about to black out.
Somewhere a family, a girlfriend, prepared for his return.
Somewhere a telegram raced toward them into Pacific Time
and the dark that rose like water in his room.

Taken from *The Moon Reflected Fire*

How to Pray

D E B O R A H   D E N I C O L A

Softly at first. Like a peony
drugged in her own concoction of dizzy light,
emitting a steady aroma into the drone
of the late summer bees.
Then with the languor of autumn

leaves, that yawn into yellow, bowing your head
like a dying aster, each erect blue star,
a vibrating tine
finding the OHM of the cosmos
tuned to the blue rain, your voice—

rich as the splashy evening dress
on its stolen hotel hanger,
each lamé eyelid, a haloed shower of gold
and the night in the window,
those velvet folds, ululating chaos.

Then as the skin on the knees winces louder,
you're grappling visibly
with the minted coming of words,
sounding your nouns with their open vowels
propelled by feverish verbs—

And finally, on your feet, at an earthshaking pitch,
shouting the clouds into laurels, webbing
the haunted heavens, priding yourself on the sheer
lusciousness of your raw supplications

for shelter, sustenance, love
no pain-making god in his good mind could resist.

Taken from *Where Divinity Begins*

Washing Beans

RITA GABIS

I love the feel of beans in water,
beautiful in the colander, bright as stones
after low tide is over and the salt wash rises
and covers the sides they bare to the moon.
The skins split from the red ones and wrinkle,
the round black ones might have fallen from a star.
I could pray to the white ones, they are so ordinary.
I think of each bean as a life, we were born
in the same field, between two poles,
two extremities of cold. I live for simple things,
the lump under one arm that is nothing;
oil from sweat the doctor said, life isn't meant
to be easy. I stand at the sink, my hands covered with
three kinds of beans. This is the anniversary
of my friend's death. I remember his last haircut.
He didn't feel the universe resting on his shoulder,
the seed start to split, the skin pull back from the bones
until the soul wandered out. I don't have the heart to say
beans have no meaning. They will not be lost to me.
They might be the eyes of the wind, they might be kidneys.
They have no ghosts, but they have shadows, and come back
as roots or the gourd's armor or stone.

Taken from *The Wild Field*

After You Died

RICHARD McCANN

I had a body again. And I could recall
how it had been, back then,

to want things. Easy to recall that now—
this sun-dazed room; lilacs, in white bowls.
But for a long time I was grateful
only for what your dying was taking from me:
the world, dismantling itself; soon there'd be no more obstinacies,
I wouldn't want anything again . . .

After you died I rode a bicycle around the lake all day, in circles.
I had come back. And so it was hard not to remember
how it had been walking the path that circled the lake
where I'd once gone each night to look for sex.
It's true that I drank heavenly

—*heavily*, I mean. I was drunk.
I walked until someone wanted me. But what did I hope
to love in return?—I followed him, his pale shirt disappearing
into a small clearing hidden by shrubs.
He undressed, his bare chest mottled by moonlight's shadows of leaves.
If I could have followed you like that, even in grief,
into a clearing littered with wadded paper tissues

                                            —white carnations!
Mostly I met no one.
The path ended by the public toilets.
I loitered by a row of urinals; or I stood outside,
beneath the dim, caged streetlamp,
in a body I hated. Without it,
who'd need to ask the world for a thing?

Taken from *Ghost Letters*

One of the Reasons

RICHARD McCANN

The street is
a cathedral, even better
because the storefronts' brick
vaulting returns
my eye to earth. While the lame
girl's lame leg's fluttering
her blue skirt, her mother
yanks her hand, says
Come on
which is not so bad as it might sound and is
maybe a kind of prayer, after all: irregular
gait & words, they
walk that way, don't
get me wrong. There are

lots of junk stores open. Floating
on the lake of a blue-mirrored
Art Deco table a wicker bait basket
overflows with lures: little radiant
fish, metallic lights
barbed with hooks, who would not
want to eat you? I am so easily
convinced by things—by *things*, I mean—
I am fluttering, a blue skirt
ruffling like a lake. Rhythm
means fr. RHEIN to flow—more
at STREAM. Imagine

how many things there are to buy and imagine
you would never get tired of buying them—
not just the anthurium in the slender Steuben vase
but also house slippers, bok choy, fleshy pink

bunion pads, linguini, Sardo, birds'
shadows on sidewalks, the whole
painted-over storefront
of the Holiness Pentecostal Church.

This is just
one of the reasons
I like
certain poems, the old lady
right now perilously
crossing the street
against traffic, the weighted
left pocket of her
unseasonable cloth coat
against which the rich
secret
of her handbag
strikes.

Taken from *Ghost Letters*

Resurrection

FORREST HAMER

You think you might die. You think you've stopped breathing

and you might die; yet, your eyes don't leave his face,
you let him kiss the stretch of your neck,
you smell each other. This you do

until you give breath back
which no longer belongs to the same life,

which is a blessing.

Taken from *Call & Response*

No Stone

E.J. MILLER LAINO

marks the grave, still
I call out, expecting
her hand to push
through
the shifting earth.
(it's summer, it's soft)
She could do it, a mother
can do anything. I would stop running
my fingers through the blades
of grass, smoothing them down
the way a mother moves her whole hand
over the smooth head of her baby.

Even if every mother, alert
under the tumbling earth
was listening for her daughter's call,
(it's soft, it's summer)
and shot her hand through the parting
ground, I would know the swollen finger
joints, the bent knuckles.
I could find my mother's hand
in the middle of millions, waving
back and forth, in perfect time
with the swaying grass.

I could hold
my mother's hand
(it's summer, it's soft)
until the orange sun
sets itself.

Taken from *Girl Hurt*

The Mouth of Grief

ROBERT CORDING

I remember how we stood there,
In that poorly lit church in Arezzo, straining
With binoculars to see *The Legend*, half worn away.

All afternoon we studied how Francesca added one scene
To the one before until it told the story

Of the True Cross,
Each fresco a signpost pointing the way
Of a past made and corrected and made again,

Without end, as though we were always bound
To discover our innocence was already marked.

We kept coming back to an old Adam
Staggering under the weight of his being.

Even after he has been laid down,
His children cannot understand their father's implacable gaze.

Unimaginable. Unimaginable, that first death
Until Seth, gone for oil of mercy, returns with a branch
From the Tree of Knowledge.

Until that one child finds her mouth opened
Against the silence of a face turned away.

From her mouth,
Those first wild involuntary words must enter
The stricken landscape

No one has ever finished restoring,
Their deep syntax of grief

Something we must have understood even before
We could speak it.

Taken from *Heavy Grace*

The Cup

ROBERT CORDING

What longing you had to be nothing more
Than the light moving
Across the grass like the stateliest ship.
To move into a light you could not glimpse.
How many times in the dark
Too dark to see in, death came to you,
A weightless lover, and unraveled its beautiful oasis
Out of nothing for you.
And each time you must have thought, "It is right
That I go away and not return."

And yet, after the days
Had lost any gleam of welcome,
After sleep had become a battle
To wake to another pain, it took only our voices
To call you back. There we sat, at bedside,
Saying your name.

As though a human voice could dispel the dream
You wanted to become the world,
You stayed. Or as though you had learned
From all those years
Of sitting at dusk with neighbors,
One or two to a stoop, the close houses
Like sunstruck metal giving back the day's heat,
That there is no place else to go.
Or perhaps the cup of unhappiness you drank from
Was not emptied
Until we could say, "You must go now,
Your suffering is too much for us to bear."

Taken from *Heavy Grace*

The Book of God

THEODORE DEPPE

St. Dympna's Hospital, 1994

I'm thinking tonight of the three times
Marisol's tried to kill herself before her sixth birthday—

long red suture lines on both arms—
and of the picture she cut from the *Newsweek*

I'd brought to read on break—I still don't know
how she got it—a photo of a crucified girl,

one of several Bosnian children nailed to the doors
of their own homes to frighten the parents away.

For Marisol she hangs there without explanation,
head bent down, black hair falling over jutting ribs.

The single spike through her blue feet
rotates her legs inward, creating a knock-kneed

pigeon-toed schoolgirl of a saint.
Around the tortured girl Marisol taped whole tulips

from the hospital garden. Sacrilege,
my taking down her bedside shrine.

Nothing I said about the photo
troubling the other children made sense:

when I took the picture from her wall
she dug her nails in my wrist, tried to bite my hand.

Only later, and reluctantly, she accepted
the spiral notepad I gave her to write about the girl.

She didn't want words inside but on the cover
she wrote in block letters THE BOOK OF GOD CAME BACK

AS A SMALL GIRL. On each page
she drew pictures she couldn't talk about.

Taken from *The Wanderer King*

Riding with the Prophet

THEODORE DEPPE

By the third night my father squints at the road
as if following faint deer tracks.
His hands shake at the wheel. By now
I know I have failed him. He won't say it
but I can hear his voice clearly: "Maps
of the outside world are nothing.
Look inside, are you listening to me?"

"No, I'm not," I think and keep on drawing.
I put down road numbers and schools, a heron
wading in the Little Wolf River, the name
of a waitress from the tag on her blouse.
But there are gaps in my map, times
I fell asleep and found he'd changed routes
again. He liked unmarked roads best.

And at the map's center, the place where I woke
and heard the lull of his voice talking to itself.
My first glimpse of the desert: a sharp moon
above his shoulder, and the shapes
of dark mountains that traveled with us.
I wake now at a truck stop, someone tapping at the glass
and my father too tired to roll the window down

and order gas. The pump-boy shrugs, swears,
walks away. Farm trucks idle, unattended, exhaust
rising above the diner. I close the door quietly, start

walking. Time again my father wakes
alone, follows my path through this red grass.
"There's going to be a new heaven," he says,
"and a new earth. Be sure you get them on your map."

Taken from *Children of the Air*

Invisible Dark

CYNTHIA HUNTINGTON

Like a black car going off the road,
turning into weeds, nudging under the bridge
into high weeds, its fins black ears
pointing backwards to hear what was said
before, going past. Like a low blue
Thunderbird black in the night
glistening, like the midnight whisper
of the engine running low, and the radio
whispering, whimpering, whispering,
whimpering, the ears laid back stroked
by down-hanging branches of willow. Soft,

like the first taste of beer, half-warm
from the can, sweet, skunky taste of it,
burn, bitter in back of the throat.
Summer night in the front seat, three
of them there and the girl, seventeen,
downing Colts; he warns and she
faster boldly swallows,
while her friend sips cautiously
lapping the edge of can, tasting foam,
aluminum, lipstick, smelling it. Stale.
How the sweat seeps out of you,
pink checked shorts, back of thighs
sticky on the plastic seatcovers
and he drops his arm across the seat back
behind his girlfriend and his hand
almost to the window caresses the knob
of the girlfriend's friend's bare shoulder.
And talking the whole while, then get out
to piss behind the car, a hand steadying
against the hot black of the bumper.

Soon they've wandered fumbling, soft , down
into weeds by the creekside; seventeen
feels sick, groans and says leave me
alone goes into the tall grass moving
like china, and sixteen in the lock
of darkness silently opens like a cloth unfolding
there in the grass, in the invisible dark,
simply falls beneath the boy and takes him in
—like *that*, completely that—it will never
be like that again, it is all lost
for good, in the invisible dark.

Taken from *We Have Gone to the Beach*

The Sign

SHARON KRAUS

for M.B.G.

He says I have a history
and that he doesn't, not really. Not
like mine. All day he's filled
the cups of our friends
with more wine, the many glasses
trembling with their sour wash. I know
he means he was not in his body molded by
the blunt print of a father's foot, that he never
lay outside his parents' locked universe
for the span of a clear night. And yet,
the idea of the print still lingers on the underside
of his torso: the perfect curve of the heel; and
the sound of the latch possibly clanging
quietly echoes even now. Doesn't it? Does he not hear
the awful hasp whisk shut? —Why
do I want him to? But here
is the tuneful wine chiming in the glasses: I love
even the look of his drink, the pale gold
bits of fruits' skins
orbiting together in the glass, how they still hold
one summer's ferocious sun. My friend sits beside me —
from the window near us, I can see
the great tree in the rain as it begins:
first one leaf shudders, then several.
Then all the leaves stir, making similar motions.

Taken from *Generation*

We Live in Bodies

ELLEN DORÉ WATSON

That we do means everything to me now
as I try to sort you out try to imagine
sticking you in the ground veins
drained or bones burned to dust try
to imagine what will be left here
in my lap empty hands mind's eye
my cup of having to go on

We live in bodies clumsy and disobedient
and we love them even as we punish
with too much or too little
we think we're bigger than they are
and then we sit dumbly surprised
how easily that tiny jot of spirit can get lost
so many folds of yellow and pink tissue

There are those who have looked back looked down
from ceilings of hospital rooms and returned to us
we see their lips full and red again but their words
hover fleshless in vowels and consonants
our heads nod yes our bones say no because living
in bodies means blood in all its horror and beauty
means making each other hum and ooze making
baby bodies means we can lay our hands on their
bodies where and when we must not
as we age our bodies pale with the knowing

The fact of sagging flesh and bodily regrets
the fact of slowly applied pain the hand somewhere
applying it while in this latitude her small mouth

tugs and closes over my nipple
the power of a shriek the solace of singing
winding our twisted sinewy streets
bodies are the doomed and wonderful cities where we live

Taken from *We Live in Bodies*

One of the Ones

ELLEN DORÉ WATSON

I will not forget the body, and that's final.
I will not forget the edge in the voice,
its intentions. I will not forget
the music on the breeze, I will be subverted.
I will not forget what's under the snow,
the bandage, the rug. I won't forget
her forgetting, how one day to fry a pork chop
was beyond her. Or that the matches lie
ready in their flowered tin beside the stove.
I will not forget that we are less
because we decided not to be more.
I won't forget you and you and you, each
with a brutal truth to send away
in a little boat, let me be one of the ones
to keep it afloat, I'll remember.
I will not forget to be defiant, ha.
I'll not forget that remembering is money
well-spent—no: money in the bank—remembering
can be certain and gentle like a mother's hand
in our sleep, a hand that knows we will move
in strange ways when we wake.

Taken from *Ladder Music*

Illumination

ADRIENNE SU

It happened in a green courtyard in Virginia.
It was summer and I was sixteen.
   Some kids I knew walked by and waved,
and I waved back, unable to move.

The moment held me there.
I felt unobtrusive for the first time
and knew that if things had happened differently,
I could disappear among them,

but—also for the first time—I had a purpose.
At once it lifted me off the concrete path
and anchored me to the ground.
                              This was to be my life.

I could go to them, but now, knowing I could,
would not. I would stand in the hot doorway
just out of the sun, and watch the light pass over the brow
of the boy I wanted to walk with,

and tell of his face and shoulders, the damp air, and the
   desire for him.

Taken from *The Middle Kingdom*

Body and Soul

B.H. Fairchild

Half-numb, guzzling bourbon and Coke from coffee mugs,
our fathers fall in love with their own stories, nuzzling
the facts but mauling the truth, and my friend's father begins
to lay out with the slow ease of a blues ballad a story
about sandlot baseball in Commerce, Oklahoma decades ago.
These were men's teams, grown men, some in their thirties
and forties who worked together in zinc mines or on oil rigs,
sweat and khaki and long beers after work, steel guitar music
whanging in their ears, little white rent houses to return to
where their wives complained about money and broken Kenmores
and then said the hell with it and sang *Body and Soul*
in the bathtub and later that evening with the kids asleep
lay in bed stroking their husband's wrist tattoo and smoking
Chesterfields from a fresh pack until everything was O.K.
Well, you get the idea. Life goes on, the next day is Sunday,
another ball game, and the other team shows up one man short.

They say, we're one man short, but can we use this boy,
he's only fifteen years old, and at least he'll make a game.
They take a look at the kid, muscular and kind of knowing
the way he holds his glove, with the shoulders loose,
the thick neck, but then with that boy's face under
a clump of angelic blonde hair, and say, oh, hell, sure,
let's play ball. So it all begins, the men loosening up,
joking about the fat catcher's sex life, it's so bad
last night he had to hump his wife, that sort of thing,
pairing off into little games of catch that heat up into
throwing matches, the smack of the fungo bat, lazy jogging
into right field, big smiles and arcs of tobacco juice,
and the talk that gives a cool, easy feeling to the air,
talk among men normally silent, normally brittle and a little
angry with the empty promise of their lives. But they chatter

and say rock and fire, babe, easy out, and go right ahead
and pitch to the boy, but nothing fancy, just hard fastballs
right around the belt, and the kid takes the first two
but on the third pops the bat around so quick and sure
that they pause a moment before turning around to watch
the ball still rising and finally dropping far beyond
the abandoned tractor that marks left field. Holy shit.
They're pretty quiet watching him round the bases,
but then, what the hell, the kid knows how to hit a ball,
so what, let's play some goddamned baseball here.
And so it goes. The next time up, the boy gets a look
at a very nifty low curve, then a slider, and the next one
is the curve again, and he sends it over the Allis Chalmers,
high and big and sweet. The left fielder just stands there, frozen.
As if this isn't enough, the next time up he bats left-handed.
They can't believe it, and the pitcher, a tall mean-faced
man from Okarche who just doesn't give a shit anyway
because his wife ran off two years ago leaving him with
three little ones and a rusted-out Dodge with a cracked block,
leans in hard, looking at the fat catcher like he was the sonofabitch
who ran off with his wife, leans in low and throws something
out of the dark, green hell of forbidden fastballs, something
that comes in at the knees and then leaps viciously towards
the kid's elbow. He swings exactly the way he did right-handed,
and they all turn like a chorus line toward deep right field
where the ball loses itself in sagebrush and the sad burnt
dust of dustbowl Oklahoma. It is something to see.

But why make a long story long: runs pile up on both sides,
the boy comes around five times, and five times the pitcher
is cursing both God and His mother as his chew of tobacco sours
into something resembling horse piss, and a ragged and bruised
Spalding baseball disappears into the far horizon. Goodnight,
Irene. They have lost the game and some painful side bets
and they have been suckered. And it means nothing to them

though it should to you when they are told the boy's name is
Mickey Mantle. And that's the story, and those are the facts.
But the facts are not the truth. I think, though as I scan
the faces of these old men now lost in the innings of their youth,
I think I know what the truth of this story is, and I imagine
it lying there in the weeds behind that Allis Chalmers
just waiting for the obvious question to be asked: why, oh
why in hell didn't they just throw around the kid, walk him,
after he hit the third homer? Anybody would have,
especially nine men with disappointed wives and dirty socks
and diminishing expectations for whom winning at anything
meant everything. Men who knew how to play the game,
who had talent when the other team had nothing except this ringer
who without a pitch to hit was meaningless, and they could go home
with their little two-dollar side bets and stride into the house
singing *If You've Got the Money, Honey, I've Got the Time*
with a bottle of Southern Comfort under their arms and grab
Dixie or May Ella up and dance across the gray linoleum
as if it were V-Day all over again. But they did not.
And they did not because they were men, and this was a boy.
And they did not because sometimes after making love,
after smoking Chesterfields in the cool silence and
listening to the big bands on the radio that sounded so glamorous,
so distant, they glanced over at their wives and noticed the lines
growing heavier around the eyes and mouth, felt what their wives
felt: that Les Brown and Glenn Miller and all those dancing couples
and in fact all possibility of human gaiety and light-heartedness
were as far away and unreachable as Times Square or the Avalon
ballroom. They did not because of the gray linoleum lying there
in the half-dark, the free calendar from the local mortuary
that said one day was pretty much like another, the work gloves
looped over the doorknob like dead squirrels. And they did not
because they had gone through a depression and a war that had left
them with the idea that being a man in the eyes of their fathers
and everyone else had cost them just too goddamned much to lay it

at the feet of a fifteen-year-old boy. And so they did not walk him,
and lost, but at least had some ragged remnant of themselves
to take back home. But there is one thing more, though it is not
a fact. When I see my friend's father staring hard into the bottomless
well of home plate as Mantle's fifth homer heads toward Arkansas,
I know that this man with the half-orphaned children and
worthless Dodge has also encountered for his first and possibly
only time in the vast gap between talent and genius, has seen
as few have in the harsh light of an Oklahoma Sunday, the blonde
and blue-eyed bringer of truth, who will not easily be forgiven.

Taken from *The Art of the Lathe*

Keats

B.H. FAIRCHILD

I knew him. He ran the lathe next to mine.
Perfectionist, a madman, even on overtime
Saturday night. Hum of the crowd floating
from the ball park, shouts, slamming doors
from the bar down the street, he would lean
into the lathe and make a little song
with the honing cloth, rubbing the edges,
smiling like a man asleep, dreaming.
A short guy, but fearless. At Margie's
he would take no lip, put the mechanic big
as a Buick through a stack of crates out back
and walked away with a broken thumb
but never said a word. Marge was a loud,
dirty girl with booze breath and bad manners.
He loved her. One night late I saw them in
the kitchen dancing something like a rhumba
to the radio, dishtowels wrapped around
their heads like swamis. Their laughter chimed
rich as brass rivets rolling down a tin roof.
But it was the work that kept him out of fights,
and I remember the red hair flaming
beneath the lamp, calipers measuring out
the last cut, his hands flicking iron burrs
like shooting stars through the shadows.
It was the iron, cut to a perfect fit, smooth
as bone china and gleaming under lamplight
that made him stand back, take out a smoke,
and sing. It was the dust that got him, his lungs
collapsed from breathing in a life of work.
Lying there, his hands are what I can't forget.

Taken from *The Art of the Lathe*

Airlifting Horses

B.H. FAIRCHILD

Boy soldiers gawk and babble, eyes rapt
in what seems like worship as the horses rise
in the bludgeoned air. A brush fire is swarming
roads and highways, and the last way out is up

or a flatboat in the lagoon. We used to drop
the reins and let them race there, hurdling
driftwood, heaps of kelp, waves lapping the sand
in a lace maker's weave of sea and foam.

Now they're startled into flight, and the air,
stunned and savaged by the propeller's flail,
beats us back. Its sudden thunder must be a storm
their skins have for the first time failed to sense.

Cowering beneath the blades, we have cradled them
like babies, strapped them in slings strong enough
to lug trucks, and their silence is the purest tone
of panic. Their great necks crane and arch,

the eyes flame, and their spidery shadows,
big-bellied and stiff-legged, swallow us,
then dwindle to blotches on the tarmac
as they lift. The cable that hauls them up

like some kind of spiritual harness vanishes
from sight. Their hooves pummel the heavy wind,
and the earth they rode a thousand days or more
falls away in hunks of brown and yellow.

Even the weight of their bodies has abandoned them,
but now they are the gods we always wanted:
winged as any myth, strange, distant, real,
and we will never be ourselves till they return.

Taken from *The Art of the Lathe*

from the archives of

ALICE JAMES BOOKS

Aug 14, 1980

Dear Alice,

I am having a grand summer here on Vinalhaven Island which is where we really should have the summer institutes. Of course a little hard to reach....

I hear this year's went well— I was sorry to miss it. I was especially disappointed to miss Maxine Kumin's reading. I studied with her a semester at Brandeis and she was a very very good teacher.

My health has taken a turn for the better. Now I feel completely well. I am very much looking forward to returning in the fall and this year plan to come back and do some work in the office. I have not forgotten zip codes. I plan to look for work, but hope to work part-time.

Could someone (hello) kindly send ⑤ copies of my book to me here in Maine? I have none with me (after wedding, trip to England I hardly had time to catch my breath and none to think) Here's a check for $20.00 which should cover— if not, let me know. See you all soon. My thoughts are never very far from you/us.

Love, Beatrice (Hawley)

Box 147
Vinalhaven, Maine 04863

Letter from Beatrice Hawley to AJB, 1980.

Postcard from Willa Schneberg to AJB, 1980.

1980

Top: Jane Kenyon, Frances Fremont-Smith,* Margo Lockwood, Robert Louthan,
         Joyce Peseroff, Nina Nyhart, Helena Minton
Center: Kinereth Gensler, Ruth Whitman, Marjorie Fletcher, Connie Veenendaal,
         Jeffrey Schwartz, Elizabeth Knies
Bottom: Kathi Aguero, Ruth Buchman,* Alice Mattison, Ruth Lepson
*: Office Manager

A gathering of Alices, 1980.

Betsy Sholl and Jean Pedrick during the early years of AJB.

1983

Top: Robin Becker, Ruth Lepson, Marie Harris, Cathy Hawkes,* John
Hildebidle, Susan Snively, David McKain, Beatrice Hawley,
Margo Lockwood
Bottom: Ruth Whitman, Frances Fremont-Smith, Marjorie Fletcher, Celia Gilbert,
Miriam Goodman

Alices, 1983.

Photo credit: Jonathan Deitz

Five of the seven founders of AJB: Cornelia Veenendaal, Jean Pedrick, Marjorie Fletcher, Patricia Cumming, and Lee Rudolph. Not pictured: Betsy Sholl and Ron Schreiber, 1973.

Marjorie Fletcher sets type on the first AJB books, 1973.

Cornelia Veenendaal and Marjorie Fletcher work on the first AJB books, 1973.

The Power Table

You, lying across the wide bed, vertical,
I, horizontal,

~~I for~~ you, I, in a green field two green paths
flowered with xxxx's and xxxx's

you, I, lined inside
with pre-historic gravels

old black cuts
in a wooden kitchen table

the table where you sit down with your older brothers
the table where things get settled once 4 for all

the cow's hip shaved down to the brand
her body divided into zones.

Yes I am standing in the doorway
yes my softness 4 my hardness are filled with a secret light,

but I want world-light
and this-world company.

for   The River at Wolf
      Jean Valentine

"The Power Table" draft by Jean Valentine for *The River at Wolf*.

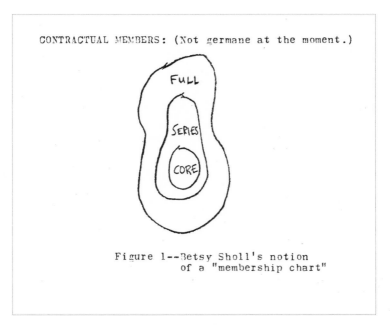

CONTRACTUAL MEMBERS: (Not germane at the moment.)

FULL

SERIES

CORE

Figure 1--Betsy Sholl's notion
of a "membership chart"

Early "membership chart" drawing by Betsy Sholl, 1973.

June 11, 1977

Ruth Whitman
1514 Beacon Street
Brookline, Mass. 02146

Dear Ruth--

Welcome home! I understand that you'll be back Monday, and
since Walter and I are going off to New York for a few days (back
Wednesday morning), I wanted to be sure to get this into the mail
before I take off.

It makes me very happy to be able to tell you, on behalf of
Alice James Books, that Tamsen Donner has been accepted for publi-
cation, and to welcome you as a member of the Alice James Poetry
Cooperative. You know how much I believe in that manuscript, having
watched it grow and change and deepen. We have not yet set a publi-
cation date, but by the end of this week should have a much better
idea of our over-all schedule. Somewhere along the line there'll be
a welcome to new authors (& work schedule) meeting--probably late
summer or Labor Dayish. Also, somewhere along the line, there'll
be an AJ contract to sign.

Meanwhile, this has got to be a great way for you to re-enter
the U.S.A.! Just received a letter from Avima, who said she'd seen
you both. Am looking forward to your report.

Love and congratulations,

Kinereth Gensler, for alicejames

P.S. The one editorial comment I ought to pass along was the feeling
that where Tamsen's own letters were used, that should be so
indicated.

Letter to Ruth Whitman from Kinereth Gensler on behalf of the
Cooperative, 1977.

One Meadway

"Jean Valentine opens a path
to a mature place where
there is "no inside wall":
rapturous, risky, shy of
words but desperately true
to them, these are poems
that only she could write."
                    Seamus Heaney

Handwritten blurb by Seamus Heaney for Jean Valentine's *The River at Wolf*,
circa 1992.

WRITING PROGRAM
DEPARTMENT OF HUMANITIES
MASSACHUSETTS INSTITUTE OF TECHNOLOGY
CAMBRIDGE, MASSACHUSETTS 02139
(617) 253-7894

26 May 1981

Dear Alice James Folks,

I'm delighted to accept the offer of publication for my manuscript _All Chemistry and Vapors_, and to hear that you liked the book so much.

I look forward to seeing everyone in the fall!

Have a good, productive summer,

Sincerely,

Robin Becker

Note from Robin Becker on the acceptance of her manuscript, _All Chemistry and Vapors_, 1981.

J
Miriam Goodman
7 Buena Vista
Cambridge, Mass. 02140   November 9, 1981

Dear Miriam;

You weren*t at home at 3:30 to hear the news from all of us
in concert that we love the manuscript and the answer is YES.
We would love to publish it next fall, 1982.

We have some changes we would like you to make. We hope you
will agree: the title, the order, and possibly replacing the
prose pieces.

Just call anyone of us seven who were the manuscript committee
and we can talk about it.

                            Sincerely,

                            Kinereth Gensler
                            Ruth Whitman
                            Ruth Lepson
                            Allice Mattison
                            Susan Snively
                            Liz Knies
                            Margo Lockwood

P.S. We hope to see you at the next monthly meeting (Nina Nyhart*s
house, Sunday, December 5 -- time about 1:00, I think).

Letter from the Cooperative to Miriam Goodman accepting her manuscript,
Signal::Noise, 1981.

Contact sheet of Alices in action, 1983.

Women Poets Share Chores at Alice James Books

Special to The New York Times

CAMBRIDGE, Mass. — They count among themselves Fulbright and Bunting Institute scholars, winners of the Pushcart Prize, the Poetry Society of America Prize, the Discovery Award from the 92d St. Y in New York and prizes from 12 states.

They publish their own books without cash advances or royalties. They design the covers and oversee production, publicity and distribution. When they make a sale from their Harvard Square office, they type the invoice and may even hand-deliver the book.

They are the poets of Alice James Books, an author-run press that emphasizes works by women and has published 52 volumes. Last month, the press celebrated its 12th anniversary of publishing only poetry.

The founding poets — five women and two men — assumed the name of the troubled, 19th-century diarist who was the sister of the prominent psychologist William and the novelist Henry. Although Alice James traveled in literary circles, living in New York City; Newport, R.I.; Cambridge, Mass., and Europe, she began to write only three years before her death at the age of 43.

Henry James considered Alice's diaries, her only writing, an invasion of family privacy, and he burned his copy, according to the biographer Leon Edel.

"Clearly, Alice had talent she couldn't develop because she didn't have the support we want to offer women writers," said Marjorie Fletcher, the only one of the seven founders who has been continually active at the press.

Four Volumes a Year

Since 1973, Alice James Books has published two volumes each spring and two each fall, usually 1,000 copies per printing. Each book is 72 pages, 5 by 8 inches, produced for $3,000 and costs $12.95 in hardcover and $6.95 in paper. Half of the press's $30,000 annual budget comes from sales, half from grants, most recently from the National Endowment for the Arts, the Massachusetts Council for the Arts and Humanities and the New England Foundation for Artists.

Alice James members — authors the press has published or plans to publish — select the titles to be published between February and April of the year before publication. New members sign a two-year contract with the press, agreeing to undertake many of the tasks needed to bring a raw manuscript to the bookstore shelf.

"My real life as a writer started when I joined Alice James," said Ruth Whitman, a Harvard instructor, a Fulbright and Bunting scholar who had published with two other presses before going to Alice James in 1976. Her book "Tamsen Donner" has been the Alice James best-seller at 4,000 copies.

"With Alice James set up as a cooperative for poets, not a vanity press, we own all aspects of our copyright," Miss Whitman said at a party celebrating the press's 12th anniversary. "It keeps the book in print while big presses destroy unsold copies after a few years. In lieu of royalties, we get 100 books, which are worth more than the money we'd get from most publishers."

Alice James also offers intangibles, according to Elizabeth Janeway, a New York novelist, critic and arts administrator who was guest speaker at the anniversary party. "There's a built-in system of peer review and collaboration," she said. "The kind of thing literary groups used to do 100 years ago."

'Instant Community'

Fanny Howe, who teaches at M.I.T. and wrote 16 books before she signed with Alice James, said the press provides a community spirit for writers.

"Writers are such awfully selfish people, but suddenly you're not when you join this instant community," she said in an interview at the press's office, which consists of two rooms and a walk-in storage area.

Celia Gilbert, winner of a Pushcart Prize and a Discovery Award, said the press offered the chance to shed the writer's customary isolation. "Doing the work ourselves sharpens our sense of what it means to have our words in the public domain," she said.

Next spring, Alice James for the first time will publish a poet who lives outside New England and, therefore, won't be able to work for the press. To cover the cost of extra help, Alice James has set up the Beatrice Hawley Award, which will be financed by a grant from the National Endowment of the Arts.

"This will also enable us to publish New England poets whose time or financial constraints preclude their working at the office," Miss Fletcher said. In the future, Alice James hopes to publish anthologies and sponsor poetry readings and workshops.

Alice James authors, who range in age from the 20's to the 60's and include men as well as women, reflect the styles of different generations. "But the issues we write about tend to be universal — the need for intimacy, family and freedom," said Miss Fletcher. "On the street you see the surface, things that differentiate us; in poetry, you see an exposed soul."

Joint effort: From left, Fanny Howe, Ruth Whitman and Marjorie Fletcher at Alice James Books, an author-run press in Cambridge, Mass., which serves as a cooperative for poets.

The New York Times/(Sarah Putnam)

The New York Times article on Alice James Books, 1985.

Dear Jane – Congratulations on the NHWP award !!

I hope your health is

PO Box 203
Barrington, NH 03825
603/664-7654
FAX: 603/664-9100
October 21, 1994

improving — it's an outrage

what life deals us sometimes — I think of you often .

With love,
Marie

Dear Alices:

Great news! Poets & Writers magazine has assigned me to write an article on the history of AJB. About time, no? They did tell me they were backlogged, so I don't know when it will actually see print, but they want it right away nonetheless. So I'd like to impose upon you to fill out the following questionnaire and get it back to me by mail or FAX by November 4th. Thanks!   Marie

Name: (may I use it if I quote you?): *Jane Kenyon (sure)*
State you live in: *N.H.*
Name (s) of your AJB books: *From Room to Room*   *Yaay*
Number of other presses that have published your work (in any genre): *2/ Graywolf*
Your most important awards: *Guggenheim,*
During what years were you an active AJB member? *77 & 78*
How did you discover AJB? *through Joyce Peseroff*

What elements of the AJB process interest you most?
Its ongoingness. It is like a compost — the particulars differ from year to year but the pile keeps on cooking!

What do you see as the drawbacks to a cooperative?
It is slow, always in danger financially, and relentlessly politically correct!

What do you see as the advantages?
meeting wonderful people, learning to make and distribute books; for me, becoming familiar w/ Boston.

A few sentences that sum up your personal experience with the Press.
(How has it affected your career? Your relationships with the writing community? Your understanding of the editorial/design/production/marketing processes? What did you bring to AJB? What did AJB bring to you?   Things like that)

I came into a group of marvelous individuals who had lots of healthy aggression. It was ok to be ambitious. We cheered each other on.

What are your thoughts about AJB's affiliation with UMF?
I'm not well-enough informed about it to hazard an opinion.

What new directions would you like the Press to explore?
Just stay alive; that's all I ask

(Answer as many or as few of the above questions as you'd like. Please feel free to add comments and anecdotes on the back.)

Can you respond? Call instead if you'd like.

AJB questionnaire completed by Jane Kenyon for *Poets & Writers* article, 1994.

Handwritten note from Jane Kenyon to Marie Harris, 1994.

The MacDowell Colony Fellows
100 High Street
Peterborough, New Hampshire 03458

9/1/99

Dear Peg,

Please excuse the handwriting, but I'm at the MacDowell again with nothing but pen and paper. You had said that Alice James might be interested in re-issuing my tragic first book, "The Arrival of the Future," which won the Swallow's Tale competition back in 1985. As I've said before, unbeknownst to me, the press was going under, and the book was very badly produced and poorly distributed and might as well have been tossed into the Grand Canyon.

Of course, it would thrill me to have Alice James bring it back to life, especially since—given the past year—it might get some attention this time. Well, here's hoping.

I've sent a photocopy since so few of the books remain (I only have four myself). Don't hesitate to contact me here if you need to. I will be back in California October 3. Thanks.

Pete

Handwritten letter from B.H. Fairchild to AJB, 1999.

21 June 1975

Kinereth Gensler
45 Gale Road
Belmont, Ma. 02178

Dear Kinereth,

I'm writing to tell you how delighted, how very happy we are that you have decided to publish a collection of your poems from SOMEONE IS HUMAN in one of our projected new books of three poets together. Your interest in doing this give us great confidence in the idea.

As Jean told you on the phone Thursday, we are not yet completely set in our arrangements, but we will do our utmost to have you published this coming winter, especially since Jean, who is scheduled then, hopes to have your work appear at the same time. She is planning to meet with you soon to start discussing details and will welcome your ideas about the design of the book.

For now we'd like to keep your manuscript to study, and we'll be in touch with you as soon as we have specific information about the publication. Please phone us if you have questions, meanwhile.

Thank you for your perceptive and generous comments about our reading at the New England Poetry Club. I've made a photostat to keep.

I look forward to seeing you again and to having you with us.

My very good wishes,

Connie Veenendaal
for Alice James Books

Manuscript acceptance letter to Kinereth Gensler from Cornelia Veenendaal on behalf of the Cooperative, 1975.

II.

by Kinereth Gensler

At the age of 42, after a hiatus of twenty years, (bearing and raising children, total immersion in community affairs), I started to write poems again. Re-entry involved a prolonged and utterly absorbing apprenticeship. Then I began to publish. A child of my own times, I carried over from the '40s a belief that the only worthwhile, 'real' publication was by established commercial and university presses. It was to magazines of this ilk that I submitted individual poems and it was to such book houses, eventually, that I circulated my completed manuscript.

Because of a fortuitous, almost chance encounter, the book was accepted by Alice James before I had exhausted the list of commercial poetry publishers and before I had time to examine my own motives and needs. Unlike many Alice James authors, therefore, I had no prior commitment to alternative presses, nor was I actively searching for the shelter and support of other women writers. What I wanted was to be approved and accepted by an editorial board, parent figures who would hand me my shining book.

It never occurred to me that I could have equal status in this publishing venture. Or that I would want to participate, might even welcome it. Like the standard '40s view of marriage, I had not thought much beyond the first ceremony of being an author. Me, controlling the production aspects of my book? Actively involved in promotion and sales? What did I know about such things? The idea

Untitled article by Kinereth Gensler, circa 1978.

was odd and only faintly appealing. Mostly, it was scary. I was unprepared for the expanded horizons, the education in competency that awaited me as a member of a nonprofit women's poetry cooperative.

Actually, the most familiar aspect of Alice James was its non-profit cooperative nature. I'm used to such cooperation among women, I've always relied on it--it's what makes the world go round.. The rest of the press experience has been a revelation.

Take, for example, the right to determine what your book will look like, its physical aspects. Subject to approval by the group, Alice James poets decide for themselves what typeface and size to use for their books, what kind of paper, cover design, photographs, over-all format, etc. The quality of the finished product is within their own power to control. Having gone through this careful production process with Threesome Poems, I have learned enough to view poetry books from other houses with a newly critical eye. It is a good feeling, the beginnings of an unlooked-for (and therefore doubly welcome) competency.

Then there is the phenomenon--important to me--of Alice James Books as a 'real,' successful small press. Successful, that is, by any standard except that of money. Because members of the co-operative work for 'nothing,' receive no royalties. All monies received are used for office expenses and production costs for the next two books. How do you measure success if money is not the yardstick? You begin by examining what it is that you want from your publisher, and what it is that you hope for from the publication of your book of poems.

Royalties are the least of it. Even publication by the most prestigious of houses is primarily important for its ability to bring you maximum exposure. Exposure is what you want: for the poems, and for yourself as a poet. Exposure will bring you a readership from whose understanding, admiration, love, etc. will flow all manner or nourishing wonders.

By the test of exposure for its authors, Alice James fares surprisingly well. The standard run for an Alice James book is 2,000 copies--a goodsized run for a book of poetry. Distribution is nationwide, directly or through jobbers and distributors, to bookstores and libraries as well as to individuals and series subscribers. The books are promoted through regularly updated catalogues, promotional mailings, sales at book fairs, and occasional ads. Reviews of Alice James books have appeared quite regularly--not only in newspapers and magazines, but also in trade publications such as Publishers Weekly, Library Journal, CHOICE and KLIATT, a publication for highschool librarians.

And there are other benefits: readings, lectures, articles, teaching engagements. If there is any money to be found in the pursuit of poetry, this is where it lies.

Finally, as a member of this supportive women's press cooperative, I know what "my publisher" does for me. At any given moment I can check out my book's welfare: how many copies were sold, to whom, where the reviews have come from, whether the book has been adopted for classroom use. As it moves into the "back list," I see how it benefits from clustering with other Alice James books in an actively circulated catalogue (I help to circulate it, I help to update it). The other books are by poets with whom I have worked, who have become my friends, whose work I admire.

I go into the office as often as I can. It is a happy and calm place (we have no telephone). Whatever time and energy I have available, I try to put back into Alice James.

alicejamesbooks
published by the alice james poetry cooperative,inc.

From Robin Becker
7 Buena Vista Pk
Camb MA 02140

138 Mt.Auburn Street, Cambridge, Massachusetts 02138 617-354-1408

A QUESTIONNAIRE FOR ALL AJ MEMBERS CONCERNING AN AJ ANTHOLOGY

1. Should there be an Alice James Poetry Anthology to celebrate our 15th year, coming out in fiscal year 87-88, and in place of two books?

    yes

2. Should the anthology include all forty-five authors?

    yes

3. Should it include published work and/or new work?

    new work only

4. Should each author submit 10 pages of poems?

    yes

5. Should the final selection be made by an editorial committee?

    yes

6. Would you like to serve on that committee?

    yes

7. How many pages? 300? Including half-page photos? Statement of poetics?

    300 sounds good. ½ page photos is a nice idea.
    Statement of poetics should become incorporated into

8. Should there be a hard cover and paperback edition? *Introduction.*

    no. just softcover

9. What other questions would you like to consider?

    Writing a significant introduction seems to me to be
    of major importance.

10. Will the Marketing Committee do a comparative study of recent anthologies and prices?

                                        PRODUCTS AND SERVICES COMMITTEE
    Signed: *Robin Becker*   *Betsy Sholl P.B. Whitman*
                                        Margo Lockwood Kinereth Gensler

Anthology questionnaire completed by Robin Becker, 1987.

MARJORIE FLETCHER

63 ORCHARD STREET
CAMBRIDGE, MA 02140
(617) 547-4429

October 15, 1991

Kinereth Gensler, Clerk
Alice James Poetry Cooperative, Inc.
33 Richdale Avenue
Cambridge, MA 02140

Dear Kinereth,
    As you know, over the past few years language courses and travel to Asia have kept me away from Cambridge for increasingly long periods of time. Now I am planning to be out of the area for a least nine months. Because of this, I have reluctantly reached the conclusion that I can no longer serve as President of Alice James Poetry Cooperative, Inc., and I write to inform you that effective immediately I must withdraw as an active member of the Cooperative.
    My participation in the cooperative over the past twenty years has been central to my life, and it has been difficult for me to arrive at this decision. I will miss my involvement, the community, the sense of purpose that I found at Alice James for so many, many years. The Cooperative will, of course, always have my fullest support.

    Very truly yours,

Marjorie Fletcher

Resignation letter from Marjorie Fletcher after eighteen years with the Cooperative, 1991.

Kinereth Gensler
45 Gate Road
Belmont, Ma. 02178

Dear Kinereth,

I'm writing to tell you how delighted, how very happy we are that you
have decided to publish a collection of your poems from SOMEONE IS
HUMAN in one of our projected new books of three poets together.
Your interest in doing this give us great confidence in the idea.

As Jean told you on the phone Thursday, we are not yet completely
set in our arrangements, but we will do our utmost to have you pub-
lished this coming winter, especially since Jean, who is scheduled
then, hopes to have your work appear at the same time. She is planning
to meet with you soon to start discussing details and will welcome
your ideas about the design of the book.

For now we'd like to keep your manuscript to study, and we'll be in
touch with you as soon as we have specific information about the
publication. Please phone us if you have questions, meanwhile.

Thank you for your perceptive and generous comments about our reading
at the New England Poetry Club. I've made a photostat to keep.

I look forward to seeing you again and to having you with us.

My very good wishes,

Connie Veenendaal
for Alice James Books

Letter from Beatrice Hawley to AJB Alices, 1984.

ALICE JAMES BOOKS: THE FIRST DECADE

Marjorie Fletcher

ALTHOUGH ALICE JAMES BOOKS became a legal entity on May 18, 1973, the combination of ideas and events which culminated that day in the formation of the "writers' cooperative with an emphasis on publishing poetry by women" began in the late sixties and early seventies when feminists in many areas of the country were banding together to publish women's literature. Then Daughters Inc. began issuing novels by women. The Feminist Press was established. Alta was printing Shameless Hussy titles in northern California. Know Inc. was forming in Pennsylvania. The Naiad Press was starting in Missouri, the Women's Press Collective in Oakland and Diana Press in Maryland. In New York City the editors of *MS. Magazine* were preparing their first issue for the newsstands. In Cambridge, however, we were largely unaware that similar schemes were hatching elsewhere when we began to discuss the possibility of publishing books.

The poets who attended those early discussions had met in workshops for several years and had run a reading series that presented one hundred poets in performance. It was after printing two small anthologies in conjunction with this series that we started to dream about book publishing. For over a year the five women and two men who later formed Alice James Books met to consider the project. The precepts established during this period by the founding members have determined the unique character of Alice James Books and have been its foundation. We agreed that the press would have two major objectives—power for women and power for authors—then named the new venture for a bright, articulate woman who was unable to develop her writing talent. The majority of the work that the house would publish would be by women authors: to date the press has issued forty-six volumes, and all but six of our authors are women. We also determined that Alice James Books would be a work cooperative in which the writers whose manuscripts where chosen for publication would be solely responsible for running the business. All tasks would be shared by the authors and all decisions would be reached by consensus. We would be the publisher. We would seize that power.

By May 1973, volumes by the seven founders and an eighth by an undetermined author were scheduled. Books, we decided, would be issued in pairs. The press would publish four a year. My first book, *US: Women,* and *The Trans-Siberian Railway* by Cornelia Veenendaal were our initial effort. We rented a closet-sized office in Harvard Square and began raising funds.

"Alice James Books: The First Decade" by Marjorie Fletcher, originally published in *The Massachusetts Review*, Summer 1983, Vol. 24, No. 02.

Hundreds of letters announcing our intentions and offering pre-publication subscriptions to the first six titles were sent to poetry lovers, academics, friends, relatives and other writers. The money we received in response was enough to pay all production costs for the first two books.

Although all other Alice James titles have been printed in commercial shops, the interior pages of this first pair we printed ourselves on an ancient press at MIT that was available only when classes were not in session, after six o'clock in the evening. That September, once we had hired a printer for the covers and bought cartons of paper, we nervously pasted-up the poems we had typeset. Again and again we checked the alignment, the page sequence, the folio placement. Then, once the boards were photographed and the negatives stripped-in, we settled down to the tedious task of discovering each imperfection and blotting it out with opaquing liquid. Night after night we bent over light tables. Our backs ached. Our nerves frayed. Many days we saw the sun rise. When at long last, with the help of the press operator, the plates were rubbed-up and set in place, we heaved a collective sigh of relief. But when we fed our paper to the rollers, the giant press balked. It stained our sheets with black blotches. Or chewed the paper to confetti. Or printed far too lightly. We adjusted the ink flow. The press operator tinkered. Hours passed. We cursed. Were we facing defeat? No. Beautifully clear and readable sheets finally rolled off the machine. A miracle. We cheered. We had printed these poems. In January, after the books were bound commercially, we mailed out review copies and press releases. One thousand copies of each volume sat in cartons in our small office.

Because the April first issue of *Library Journal* included a short but glowing review of our new books, we were soon flooded with orders. The sales generated by this review, and by later laudatory notices in book pages and in feminist magazines, covered our overhead and the production costs of the spring books. This second pair of books also attracted favorable attention, and the combined sales of these four volumes paid for our two fall titles. By September of 1974, because my book had been reprinted and the others were selling so briskly that reprinting each was an inevitability, it was decided that all future volumes would have original runs of two thousand.

Clearly, Alice James Books was a success. Clearly, the house could publish more books. Poets living in New England were invited to submit. We read stacks of manuscripts. Three books were eventually chosen. Although new authors are informed when they join the cooperative that they will be expected to attend business meetings and share all tasks necessary for publishing, the decision about which manuscripts to accept is always arrived at by consensus and based entirely upon merit. The books selected that first year were issued in 1975. But before these titles were published, the cooperative underwent two important changes. The press received government assistance and Alice James Books became nonprofit.

The decision to incorporate as a nonprofit organization and to gain tax-deductible/tax-exempt status with the IRS was reached only after long debate and with the full realization that we were making a trade-off. Although each of us feels strongly that writers are entitled to generous royalties, as a nonprofit entity the house may not pay a percentage to poets because of IRS regulation. Instead, each member of the press receives one hundred books. Four specific benefits were obtained by this sacrifice. A far greater number of grants are available to nonprofit organizations than to privately held firms. Contributions are tax-deductible. Nonprofit businesses are exempt from taxes. But the crucial asset to the press is that nonprofit groups are accorded bulk mailing privileges at drastically reduced prices.

Approximately half of the cooperative's sales are generated by direct-mail promotion. Without the nonprofit postal rate the press would not exist today. And the numerous grants we have been awarded by the National Endowment for the Arts and the Massachusetts Council on the Arts and Humanities have enabled Alice James Books to maintain a steady publishing schedule. On average, one third of our annual operating budget is provided by public funding. The first awards allowed the press to reprint books that had sold out. Later awards were applied to first printings, promotion efforts and, eventually, freed capital with which we hired outside assistance in the office.

Even with a part-time employee, active members of the cooperative are obliged to devote many hours to office duties. Because the cooperative demands this commitment, only poets who live in the six New England states may submit their work. Once a year, usually in late winter, we read manuscripts. Luckily, not only is this region fertile, but our universities attract poets who are in residence for a long enough period to meet the cooperative's work requirement.

An author whose book is accepted must be willing to participate actively for approximately two years. These new members form the nucleus of the group that runs the house. Together with several writers who have elected to remain members beyond the requisite period, they oversee the various facets of production, keep financial records, dun bookstores for late payments, up-date the catalogues, write promotional material, arrange huge mailings in proper zip code order and perform the myriad other tasks necessary to run the business. This cooperative effort is the bedrock of the press. And the house is structured so that each new generation of authors is guided by experienced members. My involvement has continued since the press was founded. Others have remained nearly as long. Although some members are more "cooperative" than others, new authors are seldom truant because each has enormous vested interests. At Alice James Books the group and the individual are interdependent. When one succeeds, so does the other.

Recently I was asked during a television interview if the considerable demands on an author's time and energy required by the cooperative discourage many poets from submitting. The answer is no. Every reading period we are deluged with manuscripts. Not only is poetry the most difficult genre to sell to commercial publishers, but Alice James authors enjoy a degree of control and power that is not possible in traditional houses. Our members choose the artwork for their covers, select the typeface and determine the interior layout. The press releases and blurbs written at the time of publication are reviewed by the poet. Books are immediately sent to any critic or magazine the author designates, as well as to those on our office list. In order to target sales, each new member is asked to add to our extensive mailing lists of individuals interested in poetry, libraries, bookstores, women's studies programs, English departments and many others. Announcements and catalogues are mailed out by the thousands before each publication. Together, we select manuscripts, determine the print run, control book prices. And the interests of writers are always protected: our publisher is extraordinarily sympathetic.

But control over the publishing process is not the only benefit of membership. The cooperative is a reservoir of support for Alice James authors. We are friends. We talk and listen. We share our experiences and problems. Information is exchanged informally about job openings, publishing opportunities and grants for individual artists. A poet preparing a manuscript for publication can turn to peers for solid criticism. We organize workshops in which new work is tested. At meetings we regularly consider issues concerning women's writing and feminist publishing. When a feminist oriented magazine folds, when one of our members encounters sex discrimination at work or in publishing, when a thoughtful article appears about women's literature, when a new book by a talented woman is ignored by the media, when a literary journal publishes an issue that does not represent women fairly, when deserving women are not appointed to awards panels, when grants from funding agencies go primarily to male writers, each one of us is affected. Women's concerns and women's writing are of prime importance to all our members. One group met for several years to read and discuss the work of other women poets. Our authors read and lecture at women's arts festivals and events organized by women's studies programs. We are invited to appear on panels at conferences, to speak on radio and television. Bookstores, libraries, high schools and universities offer our members poetry readings. And the cooperative sponsors outside programs. For several summers Alice James held intensive poetry workshops and seminars at Radcliffe College. This winter a dance performance of Ruth Whitman's *Tamsen Donner* was presented at Harvard. The critics were enthusiastic.

Within six months of release, all our books are reviewed in at least a half dozen periodicals. Several volumes have won poetry prizes, and individual grants have been awarded to many of our authors. Every award, every favorable review is a boon to the cooperative. Each broadens the press' reputation. Some stimulate sales significantly. The cooperative regularly fills orders from Canada, England, Ireland and Australia. An English language bookstore in Paris carries Alice James titles, as do other bookstores in Europe. Almost since its inception, Alice James Books has enjoyed a national reputation. What accounts for our success? How have we endured?

Certainly, the availability of government funds and our location in a major learning center are both major factors. And since Alice James was formed at a historically propitious moment when cooperatives and women's ventures and even poetry were of general interest, our reputation was quickly established through magazine articles and book reviews. But the factor most vital to our success and endurance is that the press does not depend upon any one person but instead upon a community of authors each of whom has a personal interest in the realization of a shared ideal: the publication and distribution of poetry by women. From this combination of private goals and altruism springs the energy and dedication that explain why the press has flourished.

The central task now for American women is self-definition and the dominant theme of most writing by women today is the exploration of identity. No longer content to view our lives through the eyes of men, we claim the right to describe the world through our own perceptions and to pursue female selfhood. The charting of this new territory in fiction and poetry is the primary challenge of the eighties for women writing in this country. Certainly, the climate for women in writing and publishing has improved in the United States since Alice James Books was formed a decade ago. More women than ever before hold positions of power in traditional houses. The established review vehicles attend more often to women's literature. Bookstores maintain sections devoted to material on women. Universities have women's studies programs. But, especially in recessionary periods, commercial publishers simply are not irrevocably committed to women's work. We continue to need houses like Alice James Books that offer authors alternatives and that insure the steady publication of serious books by and about women.

MARJORIE FLETCHER is founder and president of Alice James Books.

ALICE JAMES BOOKS   – OFFICE AND PHONE NUMBER, PARTNERSHIP AGREEMENT

OFFICE:

AS IT STANDS, AND THESE ARANGEMENTS WILL HAVE TO REMAINED UN-
CONFIRMED FOR A SHORT WHILE BECAUSE THE MAN WE'VE BEEN DEALING
WITH HAS BEEN HOSPITALIZED WITH GALSTONES, THESE ARE THE PLANS:

A ROOM ON THE 5TH FLOOR OF 46 BRATTLE IS AVAILABLE FOR AJB

IT IS GOOD SIZED (PERHAPS 12' X 18')

THE ONLY DRAW-BACKS ARE

IT IS RUGLESS
IT HAS NO WINDOW
IT HAS AN AIR CONDITIONING UNIT IN ONE CORNER

FURNITURE WHICH WILL REMAIN INCLUDES: A LARGE TABLE, ONE COUCH,
2 GOOD LOOKING ARM CHAIRS, A SMALL FILE, A WASTEPAPER
BASKET

THE TAKEOVER DATE COULD BE APRIL 1ST.

I HAVE SUGGESTED $300 PER YEAR RENT, BUT I'VE NO REACTION YET

RUDOLPH HAS SEEN IT, SO HAVE I. WE RECOMEND AJB TAKES IT.

PHONE:

BUSINESS RATES ARE $12/MO. FOR 90 MESSAGE UNITS WITH A 15$ IN-
STALLATION FEE AND $25 DEPOSIT

THE COST OF A RECORDER TO MIND THE PHONE IS REALLY PROHIBITIVE

FOR 90¢/MO. ANY OF US COULD BUY A SECOND LISTING, IE IN THE
PHONE BOOK: JAMES, ALICE   227-8510 OR 862-2712 OR 227-9731 OR
ANY TWO OF THESE OR ALL THREE. THOUGH THE PHONE COMPANY WON'T
LET US LIST 46 BRATTLE FOR THIS NEW NAME (THEY'LL INSIST ON
83 PHILLIPS, 36 MOON HILL, 48 MT. VERNON) I SUGGEST THAT THIS
IS THE WAY TO TAKE CARE OF OUR PHONE PROBLEM -- TEMPORARILY.

PARTNERSHIP:

ROBERT ALLISON OF WARNER & STACKPOLE, BOSTON IS WORKING ON THIS
FOR US, THOUGH WE CAN'T GO FARTHER UNTIL THE ADDRESS IS FIRM.

Location proposal for AJB's offices, 1973.

Pregnant at the All-night Supermarket

L A U R A   K A S I S C H K E

Ozone spills over the frozen rolls, the whole

breathing surface of the earth, the whole

unnatural world. Outside, rusty water

yawns up from a well, while
the moon deeply sleeps in her

damp chemise of cheese, while

nurses at the hospital nearby
hover over babies
wearing white. So

much fresh and living flesh
out there—the fish-egg stars, Christ's
mildewed shroud—but here

not even the dim
memory of mold. Here

my hand passes over
what I once wanted to buy—all
those cold loaves and indifferent lies—and I

begin to believe there's nothing left
in this world
I could bear to eat

until, leaving, I see
a Luna Moth on my windshield.

Its wings are pale green.

Taken from *Fire & Flower*

After the Sacrifice

JANET KAPLAN

The English verb *to die* is akin to the Old Irish *duine*,
human being

And afterwards the sea befriended us,
Gave away its fish. It drank its own
Deep cup and did not pour the fishers down
Its icy throat. It always went like this.
The architect of grasses raised our corn
To the stars, the three-headed dogs howled
At the watchmen but sent us no fevers.
A woman furious with death might lift
Her eyes at night: the sky would hurl no fires
At her breast but hold its meteors clenched
Within its fist. Always afterwards, and
Until the peace gave way, between the human
And her shadow a kind of truce was made.

Taken from *The Groundnote*

The Denied

LISA SEWELL

Often I return to that room—abject,
mortified—where after weeks of quiet,
an occasional moan or singing, something fell
hard and I opened the door to find my grandmother
collapsed. All the shades were drawn and the air
had that hospital scent of medicine
and stale urine. When I tried to move her back
onto the bed, I felt her thick
frightened weight, our shared weariness
and panic but mostly fury at my parents
who had left for the day. I can't forget
how I wished I hadn't heard, how I knew even then
if I had passed her in a diner, her hair in a net,
the left lens of her glasses shattered, with her sweet roll
and black coffee and Parliament cigarettes, muttering
in Yiddish and trying to catch my eye, I would have denied
that I knew her. For years I have offered up this scene
as the touchstone of my nature, evidence
that I lack a portion of chromosome
that carries the genes for courage, human decency.
But recently, I have begun to practice
another kind of compassion and have looked back,
full of tenderness, for the girl I was, especially
for the moments when we lay on the damp
grainy floor exhausted, and with my arms
still wrapped around her impossible, mortal shape,
both of us rested, the only sound our labored breathing
and my weeping, as we waited
with a faith I have not felt again, for me
to find the strength to lift her.

Taken from *The Way Out*

Amber

AMY DRYANSKY

Inside the sugar maples' locked branches
something clear has begun
to come loose; it will be caught, held,

plied with intense heat.
I pity the pink tips of those branches,
their forced march in the dark

before the clocks catch up.
And I pity myself, swaddled bones
scraping food from the same black pot.

I hear the maples, their drip.
I watch the sky above the sap house
darken with ash, light up

with sparks as the boiling continues
into the night and the crude
outlines of the bright windows beckon.

I zip my high-necked dress up the back,
its straight silver teeth obediently close;
I'm so cold it feels like music.

Taken from *How I Got Lost So Close to Home*

The Book of the Dead, Revised for the Skeptical Reader

ERIC GAMALINDA

This could be the pitstop of the world,
dusk-lit and brooding , everyone a stranger
but their faces still uncannily familiar,
the way faces always look familiar to people
running from the past, or the law.
I could wake from a dream of saving us all,
cupping blood and wine in my hands,
or walking on water. This could be
my repertory of miracles, minor, selective,
unimpressive but to a few. I am writing to you
from the other side of the world.
Here morning comes sixteen hours late,
it comes in the wrack of the A train
whose doors open up to a Cuban emigre,
his voice hoarse from singing, his soul muscular
from too much love. I find myself always looking out
for places too quiet for my own good,
the way God is silent to let us think he isn't there.
I wonder if I'll stop believing in God someday,
if in his stead a churning fog will shield us
like a globe, half alive but not enough
to warrant supplication, just strong enough
to protect us from radiation and rain.
I am writing to say I will step out
into the flat light of noon where nothing shows
in stark relief, and I take my place among
the indifferent which whom I am duty-bound
to share a lifetime, and this world.
If I've said this before, and I believe I have,
ignore this warning, bear your life
like a legal document, believe in the cold blue air
that cradles the skull, that fills the lungs

of the newborn and coaxes it to cry.
This is something I wrote in the interstices
of living, my life looking over my shoulder
and telling me to get on with it. This is something
I will never send you, because words like *love*
and *quiet* and *afternoon* have no meaning
where you are, because they are no longer
necessary. Correct me if I'm wrong:
I've heard there are places even more beautiful
than this, with minarets of glass and smoke
and bridges that shoot into air,
and small towns where people look
exactly as they did in photographs
taken twenty years ago.

Taken from *Zero Gravity*

The Vulnerable

AMY NEWMAN

In the wasp's lineage from filament to airplane:
some grip of distance, some idea of thrust,

wicked thinness into the head wind,
hot little jaw and lifted shell.

In the earth's line from pitch to ground:
its dark address, the wells so deep they hold

like valentines the immaterial.
Delicate as secrets are the physical sciences,

dense and rare is the world's flipped skirt,
with a great wind basting and stirring its hem,

and underneath, the heart's content,
a crest of jewel, all latitude,

or its opposite:
a kind of homesickness, a disenchantment.

Taken from *Camera Lyrica*

Translation

MATTHEA HARVEY

They see a bird that is bright in both beak and feather
And call it cardinal not thinking to import the human
Kind words welcome those who stumble to shore
With the tilt of the sea still in their step salt stains
At their hems that seem to map out coastlines left far
Behind the new songs are the old absurd hopes
A woman wiping the table sings *bring me plans*
And money or fans and honey each word more
Strange yellow flowers spring up in the first lawns
Instead of whites dots of daisies how to tell what is
A weed is persistent and is to be emulated says a man
In a tavern in church the preacher lectures on Lazarus
Gesturing wildly as another boatload lurches along
A latitude is a guiding line a platitude a boring line
Chorus the children in school their slates scrawled
And smudged with sums that always seem to come to
Nothing is quite the same here a woman writes a letter
Near the lighthouse but the fog is so thick the words
Run as she writes them for a moment she can't tell
The sea spray from the fog one falls back the other stays
Suspended between two houses in the distance is a
Clothesline with a red shirt on it but she sees a bird

Taken from *Pity the Bathtub Its Forced Embrace of the Human Form*

In Defense of Our Overgrown Garden

MATTHEA HARVEY

Last night the apple trees shook and gave each lettuce a heart
Six hard red apples broke through the greenhouse glass and
Landed in the middle of those ever-so-slightly green leaves
That seem no mix of seeds and soil but of pastels and light and
Chalk x's mark our oaks that are supposed to be cut down
I've seen the neighbors frown when they look over the fence
And see our espalier pear trees bowing out of shape I did like that
They looked like candelabras against the wall but what's the sense
In swooning over pruning I said as much to Mrs. Jones and I swear
She threw her cane at me and walked off down the street without
It has always puzzled me that people coo over bonsai trees when
You can squint your eyes and shrink anything without much of
A struggle ensued with some starlings and the strawberry nets
So after untangling the two I took the nets off and watched birds
With red beaks fly by all morning at the window I reread your letter
About how the castles you flew over made crenellated shadows on
The water in the rainbarrel has overflowed and made a small swamp
I think the potatoes might turn out slightly damp don't worry
If there is no fog on the day you come home I will build a bonfire
So the smoke will make the cedars look the way you like them
To close I'm sorry there won't be any salad and I love you

Taken from *Pity the Bathtub Its Forced Embrace of the Human Form*

Planted Document

SUZANNE WISE

Thy Sad On Arm Longr Than Th Othr.
Thy Sad War Wound. Thy Sad Strtchd

By Wght of Brfcase Ovr Thrty Yars Tm.
Thy Sad H Workd N Lac Wth Jws

N Th Garmnt Dstrct. Thy Sad Mayb H Was
A Jw. Thy Sad Onc Hs Lttl Grl Playd Naz

N Th Suprmarkt, Goos-Stppng, Hl Htlrng
Untl Th Wf Slappd Hr Hard. Thy Sad Long

Aftr Th War, H'd March Th Nghborhood
Lat At Nght, Warng Hs Old Ar Rad Wardn Hlmt,

And Wpng. Thy Sad Th Day H Dd, Documnts
Wrttn N A Languag Hs Chldrn Dd Not Know,

Brok Opn and Flw As F Tormntd By A Grat Wnd.
Thy Sad Whn Hs Daughtr Pckd Thm Up, Nk Gushd

All Ovr Hr Hands. Thy Sad Th Words Burst
Nto A Thousand Tny Flams And Sh Dousd Thm

Wth A Fr Xtngushr. Thy Sad Sh Smard Th Words
On Purpos, Usng Hr Fathr's Favort Watrng Can.

Taken from *Kingdom of the Subjunctive*

Not a Cloud in the Sky

CORT DAY

Off to market. Not a cloud in the sky.
I'm hosting a flashover, right here in my head.
I am setting all the puppeteers to dancing.
And this time, there's no current in my chair.
In the work shed I'm making a dead civilization.
The fibers full of volts—my best suit.
In my dreams I run from tree to tree.
All the gods on this plain are capacitors.
I'm taking Aesop as my *nom de guerre*.
I am telling the story. I am full of light.

Taken from *The Chime*

Adjure Injure: Last Call

LIZ WALDNER

After a while the white night clouds climbed up
over the ragged edges of red-wooded ridges and came
toward the moon, and came toward the valley. Serried,
singular and slow, ribbed the moonlit sky and with the moon's light
conjured a pond ring of pink, a pattern of stay like the ocean's
in despite of its waves' constant motion, in their sailing through of sky.

To the east and beneath, the hundred year yews
and the eucalyptus bore between their blackened blues
a solitary bar, luminous, lenticular—and as I
looked I saw and saw I was able to see. Everything I want
is to be in love with the world like this, as I used to be,
to feel this seeing I now call being
and knew as the dark heart of 'me.'

Taken from *Self and Simulacra*

Circumstances

Xue Di

In the bikeshop basement, a repairman fits the
naked wheel. March, like a crazed sheep

Lovers leap longingly across Valentines
like black rain coming down in sunlight
Crowds collect, turning both directions

on cracked concrete roads. Tax money
maintains the smallest state stranded on the longest
polluted shore. Then come commercials

oozing with essence of female
pudenda. Private viruses made public
soothe the natives to stupor in sticky sheets

Fresh air aggravates craziness
We try to forget whatever we don't understand
powerless against distant antagonists. Reduced to

personal lives, we drift
dark and polluted streams
on the ground of freedom

Taken from *An Ordinary Day*

Where Breath Most Breathes

JOCELYN EMERSON

I love and do not love these splendid
sea birds battered through various
days and slipping into discoloration
in the level darknesses of late March.
Under them, the drawn waves ending
as innate friction. Ore, and undulation.
(What rigging for traveling a voyaging
field?) The summer's excavation
takes the partial and the discrete,
struck out with loud report. A tidal inlet.
Lampblack and cold fluid together.
Listen to the scale of varied day,
shaken singer, to the charred song
of the particle and of the mineral ash,
still and elemental in the whistling dark.

Taken from *Sea Gate*

Was Drunk

ALESSANDRA LYNCH

In the golden fields of Meadow Pond Elementary,
our favorite rebel game was drunk:
two bandits running to the far edge of the field
so no one would see us
losing it in the tall grass near the electric fence
that barely kept us in—a thin hair pin
for a topple of hair—bound to be loosed.
We'd stagger and tumble, fall and scream,
laughter punching our remarkable bellies out
under the tired sun—the other children far off—
in frozen punctuation
swung on their customary swings, docile in the sandbox
as we'd indulge in secret revelries,
imbibing the gold swoon of the wind
tipsy in the turning fields, we'd swagger
through saloon doors, barely able
to breathe for all our reckless delight
like twin bees hooked on honey,
our young breaths thick with yarrow-gin.
While, on the other side of the world,
you were already there, serious, posting your elbows
on mahogany, pounding down amber, barely able
to think about the meadow as it browned and spread its lavender
while we called to you from our fields
almost audible.

Taken from *Sails the Wind Left Behind*

About the Star-Nosed Mole:

ALESSANDRA LYNCH

it refused to be bedded in a poem
with the bull and hedgehog.
It refused to be the wolf in my room
and, moreover, would neither weep nor live
a third life. It would not even take
to the soil, however pushed to earth.
It was not fuel for the spade, it would not dangle
from precipice or burrow to birch-root and oak-sweat.
It would have no visitors and could not be
visited.

A mole
in a clench of dirt
(no air)
close to you, folding and unfolding the earth beneath you as you
covet what's other, what's not
and no breathing, no
forests, no imploring fist or foot,
no aster-shackled hill, no, not withstanding what it, no, not
endured, no man, not gripped like that, no how
no steam belt, no belly of dun, no rapture, no flame
no silken hide, no velvet
to claw, no ride
no ride out from my stuck self
there in the flowerpot
behind the picture plate
by the swinging seat
and its bruised slats
and its ditch.

Taken from *Sails the Wind Left Behind*

The Deer Comes Down the Mountain

SARAH MANGUSO

Now we gather worshipful.
The gears in his legs shine down.
He lifts his head.
Here he comes!
We're erecting a maypole with green ribbons.
His legs are four probes.
And his back is a ship
And his eyes are holes in the curtain.
We're eating cookies in the shape of him.
The icing is gold and silver.
He's shedding gears, here he comes tripping!
He is casting off the elastic bindings.
Now we're hanging giant flags.
The wind-up key sticks in his side like a blade.
The wind rocks him on his wheels.
Here he comes, crawling!
The bright obvious shines in his body.
Here comes the electric, the burning mystery!

Taken from *The Captain Lands in Paradise*

Want

ADRIAN MATEJKA

Bass lines like fat men squeezing into
3rd grade desks.

Coltrane's squealing right before I was born.

If not,
      a pill that makes
the music in my head stop.

Immediately, then I won't know
what I'm missing.

I want dissimilar words, hyphenated
by minty-fresh breath. What good
are words
      if no one will listen?

A way-back machine, so I can fix.

      William Shatner, circa 1967:
guest host for my 8th birthday party.

I'm wishing for mandibles, clipping
the staccato lilt.

Mandibles for tailoring a new dress.
My woman needs one.

Then, X-ray vision,
      so I can ignore
        what I wish for.

I want irrefutable skin
like Luke Cage, Hero for Hire.

In the semi-embarrassment of silence,
I want to understand

why Goya used spoons to paint
                instead of leaves.

                If nothing else—
a map with the exact location

of the crossroads, so I can believe
what I never should have known.

Taken from *The Devil's Garden*

Home Remedies

ADRIAN MATEJKA

> *How's your neck, boy?*
> *Strong I'll bet, being as*
> *you're still here after dark.*
> —A.M. JACKSON, CREAL SPRINGS, ILLINOIS

The science of hate isn't exact.
It works, like a child making
explosives with junior chemistry.
Most times, it's voodoo: hats
on beds, mirrors backwards,
the Devil beating his wife because
the sun shines when it rains. No
fact-based explanations, but tried
and true excuses. 10 pm, serving
food at a restaurant outside
DeSoto, Illinois, and A.M. Jackson
is a geneticist. When he theorized
my neck was strong, it made sense.
He said, *I was a pro in my day.*
Maker of knot doubled tight
like a fist before it breaks a rib.
Able to utilize the crook between
trunk and limb as a pulley, to snap
a neck for maximum flopping,
man no longer a man, more
a fish that forgot what water is.

Taken from *The Devil's Garden*

Eight Positions Mistaken as Love

ADRIAN MATEJKA

1. Man and woman, separated by two thousand
    miles, only what they can remember holding them
    is *quarantine*.

2. *Hibernation* can be holding hands, jellyfish rain
    coating fingers. No kissing in public.

3. Man and woman on a couch, looking conversation
    but murmuring nothing like deaf cicadas
    is called *euphonium*.

4. *Insomnia* is the muscularity of passion lost.
    It starts, he noticing the bags beneath her eyes.
    She, aware of the misdirection of his teeth.

5. *Quernicia* is a woman rubbing the smooth marrow
    of a man's palm in public when no one knows
    they are together.

6. When a man uses his tongue to check a woman's
    eye for the eyelash, it is called *sampling marmalade*.

7. A man and woman, lying down to sleep, but continuing
    to pull each other close. Turbid flesh to sinew, sinew
    to bone: *absolution*.

8. When a man and woman curve into each other, make
    a quiet topography of flesh, they become
    the *devil's apostrophe*.

Taken from *The Devil's Garden*

Psalm (Galileo)

DAN BEACHY-QUICK

Lit by suns more million-tongued than ours
    With flames   The blind eye knows
Not eclipse   being eclipse itself   and eclipse

Blinds both by earth's shadow and by glut
    Of light   as I am blind
By sight   of stars more numerous than belief

Can bear   and don't believe, I don't—
    Nor hear that glass bell beneath whose rim
The blue stars in chorus ring their orbits

Into heavenly chords   knocked by God's thumb
    To star-song and   now deafen me   and God
Is thumbless, and less   fluent with his tongue

Which once sang suns into cymbals
    Comets stretched long to knock   and rhyme
Their light with larger light

And failing fled   heat to reclaim ice
    Unutterable   on Lips
No other lips can kiss   have never kissed

I know, I've tried   with my eye
    to kiss   with my eye
Distance lisped into distance   doubled twice

And twice again—   nowhere was night
    enough of night not to see
How distant, God, you are from me

Ever becoming   Not singing, you are thought
    Thinking, *I am I am*—   to my question "Where
Am I?"   You gave me glass shard for my eye

to "Let me
    See, Lord, let me
See."

Taken from *North True South Bright*

When the Dog Is Chasing You

JON WOODWARD

Oh the night is dog enough
When the dog is chasing you
Oh the legs can't fast enough
When the dog's lambasting you

Oh the river's wide enough
When the dog's in the bank with you
Oh the hide ain't hide enough
When the dog's outflanking you

Oh the stairs don't climb enough
When the dog is sniffing you
Oh the guns ain't sublime enough
For the hell that dog is giving you

Oh no thoughts are loud enough
To swat that dog with reason
Oh no years are long enough
That dog owns every season

God said that little boys gotta run
And dogs gotta make them afraid
But I prayed to God to kill that dog
"God, kill that dog" I prayed

Taken from *Mister Goodbye Easter Island*

Nativity

LARISSA SZPORLUK

The wind, Master Cherry, the wind
The workshop is empty.

The voice, it doesn't exist.
By heaven, don't hurt me!

The wind, Master Cherry, the wind
Restrain this bit—*please,*

don't—reverse the grain;
give it a taste for flint,

something to live for, *don't!*
if living is what it is. Shave the outer

surface of its urge to wince;
down your wine; tuck yourself in

to the Tuscan silence,
like a tick in the musk of a beast

(or the puppet it used to be,
selfish, dreamy, festive,

up to the ears in the usual jelly),
and rest assured no one was born

this evening—no star, no king, no limb
of wood. It was only the wind,

what you think you heard—
the cry of a seasoned liar.

Taken from *The Wind, Master Cherry, the Wind*

In Tennessee I Found a Firefly

MARY SZYBIST

Flashing in the grass; the mouth of a spider clung
      to the dark of it: the legs of the spider
held the tucked wings close,
      held the abdomen still in the midst of calling
with thrusts of phosphorescent light—

When I am tired of being human, I try to remember
      the two stuck together like burrs. I try to place them
central in my mind where everything else must
      surround them, must see the burr and the barb of them.
There is a courtship, and there is hunger. I suppose
      there are grips from which even angels cannot fly.
Even imagined ones. *Luciferin, luciverase.*
      When I am tired of only touching,
I have my mouth to try to tell you
      what, in your arms, is not erased.

Taken from *Granted*

Aubade

CATHERINE BARNETT

Irregular song, irregular heartbeat,
anaphora's

stutter that neither
warns nor comforts:

I thought it was a man's voice
all this time, calling for help.

I thought it was a man
calling scared from the ditch.

Hopeless barking it was, a dog trapped
somewhere, and lonely—

then suddenly quiet.
Someone must have hitched her collar up,

stitched her mouth down,
or shot her dead—

how else break such pitch.

Taken from *Into Perfect Spheres Such Holes Are Pierced*

Ritual

CATHERINE BARNETT

In his bath my son looks half-
drowned,
lying so still,

his hair a scarf of weed,
his eyes closed,
and only the water breathing.

He practices
in his porcelain bed
his resting,

rehearsing
until the water takes cold
and he shivers a little against it.

Taken from *Into Perfect Spheres Such Holes Are Pierced*

The Disbelieving

CATHERINE BARNETT

We all saw how beautiful she looked
those first six months when she walked a thousand miles—
over the University Bridge

and under it
and into and out of the Arboretum
and up the hill to the sundial we circled every day

while the days got longer
and my sister more beautiful,
her red hair turning gray, a slow

turning, as if some force were braiding out the red,
and we looked at her
through veils—

veil of gray hair,
veil of hands over face,
veil of disbelief we all shared then.

The night after we picked up the ashes
she drew the brass urn into bed with her
and in the morning pulled back the blankets—

I've fallen asleep next to her
and I've awakened next to her
and every morning is every time

the mother lifting the sheet to see her child
sleeping and dreaming only the bed is empty
and the mother strips the blankets

and strips the sheets
down to the mattress made of stone.

Taken from *Into Perfect Spheres Such Holes Are Pierced*

A Black Horse Has Come to Your Sleep

SARAH GAMBITO

You call the black horse, "Father."
You are followed all your life.
There is a canyon.
There is a lighted stage.
There is a waiting audience.

Write a poem in three stanzas—described below:

1. Describe the canyon from the stage.
2. Describe the audience from the canyon.
3. Describe the stage from the canyon.
4. Make a horse run through all three stanzas.

Taken from *Matadora*

One Thousand Blossoms

FRANK X. GASPAR

Well, is it really wise to search for guidance in a small room
cluttered with books and papers, with a glass of whiskey
and a box of wheat crackers, with my eyes ticking like
the brass tide-clock on the plaster wall? When the house sleeps
huddled in the city's jasmine night? Night of a thousand blossoms
I can't name? Night of a soft marine layer, Pacific fog
hanging about a hundred yards up, a gauze, a parchment?
I am hidden thus from my duties, I can escape the moral law.
Isn't it written, didn't Lord Krishna himself say that we mustn't
relinquish the action we are born to, even if it is flawed?
Didn't he say a fire is obscured by smoke? You can't see far
into the city on a night like this, the blanket, the cool smell
of the sea, the dampness that sits like velvet on the rose bushes
and the African lilies and the fenders of the neighbor's truck.
You don't want less love—this ground has been covered before—
you want more love, even when you can't say what it means,
even though it binds you to the world, which you can only lose.
Then it is jasmine in the night, night of a thousand blossoms,
and my wife in one room breathing and my son in one room
breathing, and me in one room breathing. It's how loving this
place comes, slowly, then suddenly with great surprise, and then
vanishing again into mystery. Am I dreaming all of this? Is that
a train's long whistle riding the heavenly fog? Am I a drunk again
on holy books and the late hours? Now a car rolls down the street,
filling it with light then emptying it again. It's like that. Just like that.

Taken from *Night of a Thousand Blossoms*

Isn't It Enough?

FRANK X. GASPAR

I know, I know, I am responsible for holding the stars
in their proper spheres, I am responsible for every symbol
in my own dreams, my accidents, my coincidences. How then
to explain this torpor, this lack of breath and sunlight when all
the streets are steaming from the recent rain, and the birches and
the sycamores and the chestnut trees are washed clean of their
leaves, and the leaves lie along the curbs in drifts, and the bare
limbs are smooth with muscles and tendons, white in the sky?
Who would choose the spider? Who would get down on his
arthritic knees and choose the toad or the drowned earthworm?
I am off living beyond the normal mind again. I don't want
to give beauty back to God. What is owed is owed, what was
given was given: can't we leave it at that? I can't trust myself
to know what's expected of me. What lifts me up and makes me
buzz with splendor is not always good, nor goodness. It's too
much to bear, finally. I have to go out into the street and breathe
the newest air, the most advanced chemistry. The rain has fallen
and now it rises in a hundred fingers streaming into the afterlife.
Isn't it enough to walk under the arms of the great trees? Isn't it
enough to offer this confusion in its own chalice, for all it's worth?

Taken from *Night of a Thousand Blossoms*

Near the Heart of Happening

KEVIN GOODAN

The foal hangs halfway out
and the mare strains
but can't push anymore.
I bring a bucket of cold river water
across the field. Haboo
I say in her ear,
what the Skagit children said
when the storyteller stopped:
keep the story going.
They said it with clamor,
with hands and voices
louder each time
but I am soft with it,
cool water on her neck.
Haboo I say reaching in
where the hips have locked
as she groans and falters.
Haboo for the shanks I grab
and jerk, for the spine
popping and the hips coming free.
Haboo for the foal lying in the dirt
as the mare nudges
and cleans its body
as the breathing stops.
Haboo as the body cools
as we stay with it after
as light begins,
as I regard the still air,
the meadowlark, the weight
of its bright singing.

Taken from *In the Ghost-House Acquainted*

KEVIN GOODAN

Pigeon blood drying on the shit-spreader.
Field rough-ploughed but not yet worked.
Arterial chill strafes each tree in my eyes,
The blanched hives in the rafters, bee-less,
Scent of weeds burnt before hard rain, soft rain,
The real rain abating. Birds come close, veer—
Are you not my hawk, my furrow?
Clouds mount the far hills, the ewe ketotic
On her side beneath a fir, the soiled humps
That are the heave and thrash of winter
Dying. All I know is that the Lord does not
Arrive straightforward, but as a thin halo of flies,
Grass greening against its will.
I gather dark buds from branches
And say I too could start with fire.
That the earth could torch every blossom
If it had to, and go on.

Taken from *Winter Tenor*

Some vireos working towards rapture in distant oaks, as I taste pollen when I breathe, as last night's rain works slowly through grass. A mist that gleams the skin of everything rises from black dirt of fields, and I, a slow traveler standing near a fire that smolders and chuffs and rekindles. Every small leaf has emerged, every flower. Oxen in the front pasture shoulder the fence, chewing the last sprigs of the last round-bale from winter. Soon they will labor with earth by day, by night. I count on my hands until darkness, hum each mile of travel. A blackness smolders in my throat though I am shining. I gather my knapsack of blades, my seed, sprig of ivy between my teeth. I walk to the trees where I've lodged my chariot, my flaming nag. A covey of pigeons pass over, a wind is mounting from the west where bright squares of rapefield curtsy and right, their bones filling with marrow. Sheep graze, blat for their kin that come rucking through bramble into this hour, this light, this ardor. This.

Taken from *Winter Tenor*

Day Book

CLAUDIA KEELAN

Looked inside   An American soul An Amer

        I can soul inside

I found   An art museum

        Where my millions died

Mother Moon   Her burning robe

        3rd degreeing for the last time

Forgive   I read

        Before the book erased   My moving lips

A box of heaven   Sold!

        To a rich unloving bidder

I ride next to his chest   A chatter

        Inside cloth and smell   Atomic heart

Muffling   The verb auction

        What's left us   Attached

        & adventing

Taken from *The Devotion Field*

from Five Landscapes

Cole Swensen

One

Green moves through the tops of trees and grows
lighter greens as it recedes, each of which includes a grey, and among the
greys, or beyond them, waning finely into white, there is one white spot,
absolute; it could be an egret or perhaps a crane at the edge of the water
where it meets a strip of sand.

Taken from *Goest*

Gallery
KAZIM ALI

You came to the desert, illiterate, spirit-ridden,
intending to starve

The sun hand of the violin carving through space
the endless landscape

Acres of ochre, the dust-blue sky,
or the strange young man beside you

peering into "The Man Who Taught William Blake
Painting in His Dreams"

You're thinking: *I am ready to be touched now, ready to be found*
He's thinking: *How lost, how endless I feel this afternoon*

When will you know:
all night: sounds

Violet's brief engines
The violin's empty stomach resonates

Music a scar unraveling in four strings
An army of hungry notes shiver down

You came to the desert intending to starve   so starve

Taken from *The Far Mosque*

Polar

DOBBY GIBSON

Like the last light
spring snowfall
that seems to arrive
from out of nowhere
and not land, exactly, anyplace,
so too do the syllables of thought
dissolve silently into the solitude
of the body in thought.
Like touching your skin,
or the first time I touched ice
and learned it was really water
and that neither were glass,
so does the jet contrail overhead
zip something closed in us,
perhaps any notion of the bluer.
Glancing sunlight,
my shoulders bearing the burden
or any theory why these birds
remain so devoted
to their own vanishing.
One store promises flowers
for all your needs,
another tells you
everything must go.
One river runs like a wound
that will never heal,
one snow falls like a medicine
that will never salve,

you the Earth, me the moon,
a subject move in a direction
you desire, but for reasons
I believe to be my own.

Taken from *Polar*

Mary's Blood

ANNE MARIE MACARI

It was Mary's blood made him, her blood
sieved through meaty placenta to feed him,
grow him, though Luke wrote she was no more
than the cup he was planted in, a virgin
no man ever pressed against or urged
who could barely catch eyes with the towering
angel but felt God come to her like light
through glass, like a fingerprint left on glass;
still, it's hard to believe she never wanted
to be rid of the thing inside her, wasn't
shamed carrying him, the child's
perfect head pointing at the ground
and rubbing her cervix like the round earth
rubbing the thin wall of the sky that holds it.
All women reach the time of wanting it out
but not wanting it out, not knowing
what's coming, so she must have spread
her legs in anguish because what was inside
pressing her membranes for release
was both herself and a stranger;
and she must have cried out
as the small head crowned,
splitting her, her pelvis swung
wide to push him through the wall
of this world, till what came from her
was a child lit with her own gore,
soiled, everything open so her inside
was now outside, cracked open, it means
mother to crack open, to be rent
by what comes to replace her. Such
is love—the only way. It was Mary's
blood made him: his eyes, tongue,

his penis, her milk fattened his legs,
made hair on the crown of his head,
she grew caul to wrap him and door
to come through and nothing, not even
crying *Father, Father,* to the warped
blue sky can change it.

Taken from *Gloryland*

Little Church

ANNE MARIE MACARI

On Good Friday you call from across country
to describe crosses pushed

in wheelbarrows, penitents with mouths full of rocks.

Don't pray for me, is all I can think, my old faith
crawling sideways over

the dry earth, changing shapes, refusing the vinegar,
the sad sponge. I'm trying not

to plan ahead for love's daily resurrections—love born, slain,

reborn in the rumpled bed. When are you coming home?

You can't know how a woman wants, can't know
how forgiving her breasts

feel when finally found under their wrappings

as if they'd been waiting to be touched but didn't know it,
or how the muscular hand

of the vagina keeps calling, *enter, enter*, no matter
how long it takes you

to hear, how it then
lets go, cupping

the spittle and milk. Some days my belief is
a pale thing, like when

the blue afterbirth of love hangs
so heavy, the mouth of love

limp and open with weariness. The flesh knows
this one thing, it practices

for its own demise as when

giving birth, in and out of pain, a voice said, *This
is what it's like to die.*

As for the scolding bells,

I try not to listen, I'd rather feel my breath
rising toward you, so distant

from me, seeking the stray fairs at the nape
of your neck.

What horror would it take for me to go back
to the old words, to kneel again—

instead I lean into my pillow, my legs
slightly open, waiting

for when we meet skin to skin, having
to decide who I am

now that my gods have fallen away. Sometimes
only touch can help me

when I'm released with a cry

and returned to my loneliness. See how
the bed is a little church where

we have given up and taken back, spoken
in tongues, worshipped

and worshipped, then lapsed each night,

into oblivion.

Taken from *Gloryland*

A Soldier's Arabic

BRIAN TURNER

> *This is a strange new kind of war where you learn*
> *just as much as you are able to believe.*
>
> —ERNEST HEMINGWAY

The word for love, *habib*, is written from right
to left, starting where we would end it
and ending where we might begin.

Where we would end a war
another might take as a beginning
or as an echo of history, recited again.

Speak the word for death, *maut*,
and you will hear the cursives of the wind
driven into the veil of the unknown.

This is a language made of blood.
It is made of sand, and time.
To be spoken, it must be earned.

Taken from *Here, Bullet*

Here, Bullet
BRIAN TURNER

If a body is what you want,
then here is bone and gristle and flesh.
Here is the clavicle-snapped wish,
the aorta's opened valves, the leap
thought makes at the synaptic gap.
Here is the adrenaline rush you crave,
that inexorable flight, that insane puncture
into heat and blood. And I dare you to finish
what you've started. Because here, Bullet,
here is where I complete the word you bring
hissing through the air, here is where I moan
the barrel's cold esophagus, triggering
my tongue's explosives for the rifling I have
inside of me, each twist of the round
spun deeper, because here, Bullet,
here is where the world ends, every time.

Taken from *Here, Bullet*

The Hurt Locker

BRIAN TURNER

Nothing but hurt left here.
Nothing but bullets and pain
and the bled-out slumping
and all the *fucks* and *goddamns*
and *Jesus Christs* of the wounded.
Nothing left here but the hurt.

Believe it when you see it.
Believe it when a twelve-year-old
rolls a grenade into the room.
Or when a sniper punches a hole
deep into someone's skull.
Believe it when four men
step from a taxicab in Mosul
to shower the street in brass
and fire. Open the hurt locker
and see what there is of our knives
and teeth. Open the hurt locker and learn
how rough men come hunting for souls.

Taken from *Here, Bullet*

Phantom Noise

BRIAN TURNER

There is this ringing hum this
bullet-borne language ringing
shell-fall and static this late-night
ringing of threadwork and carpet ringing
hiss and steam this wing-beat
of rotors and tanks broken
bodies ringing in steel humming these
voices of dust these years ringing
rifles in Babylon rifles in Sumer
ringing these children their gravestones
and candy their limbs gone missing their
static-borne television their ringing
this eardrum this rifled symphonic this
ringing of midnight in gunpowder and oil this
brake pad gone useless this muzzle-flash singing this
threading of bullets in muscle and bone this ringing
hum this ringing hum this
ringing

Taken from *Phantom Noise*

Jundee Ameriki

BRIAN TURNER

Many the healers of the body.
Where the healers of the soul?
—AHMAD SHAUQI

At the VA hospital in Long Beach, California,
Dr. Sushruta scores open a thin layer of skin
to reveal an object traveling up through muscle.
It is a kind of weeping the body does, expelling
foreign material, sometimes years after injury.
Dr. Sushruta lifts slivers of shrapnel, bits
of coarse gravel, road debris, diamond
points of glass—the minutiae of the story
reconstructing a cold afternoon in Baghdad,
November of 2005. The body offers aged cloth
from an *abaya* dyed in blood, shards of bone.
And if he were to listen intently, he might hear
the roughened larynx of this woman calling up
through the long corridors of flesh, saying
Allah al Akbar, before releasing
her body's weapon, her dark and lasting gift
for this *jundee Ameriki*, who carries fragments
of the war inscribed in scar tissue,
a deep intractable pain, the dull grief of it
the body must learn to absorb.

Taken from *Phantom Noise*

Door to Heaven

CYNTHIA CRUZ

The night you left the world,
I went back to the house, that church
With the god taken out—

In father's blue plaid coat, and jet-black
Hair slicked back

Like a brother, or a summer
In the junk clinic. Back

Before you built the boat.
Before the fawn

With its star
On the forehead.

How the light collects about its temples.

And why not
Let it love me.

I spent a lifetime inside the destruction.
And like anyone, I made a world someplace else.

Taken from *Ruin*

Any Man May Be Called a Pilgrim Who Leaveth the Place of His Birth

CHRISTINA DAVIS

After the diagnosis,

I went to the first church I could find.
I don't know any prayers,

I only know songs that have god broken down into them.

The woman to my left spoke Spanish.
Everything she knew

was in Spanish and even what she didn't
was in it, even death was in Spanish.

She looked up

from her language. I looked
up from my language, so this is what is

meant by prayer.

Taken from *Forth A Raven*

How to Make the Case Against Happiness

JEAN-PAUL PECQUEUR

Offer it a bribe. Say, Happiness
why don't we take the chill ease
of this spring day and make something special,
you and I, some demiurgic cocktail
to sip as the sirens plunge
over the edge of our private peso opera.

The future adores its hometown parades,
the donkeys on bikes trailing flies.
Biting flies. Fireflies. Suggest fireflies.

Say, Happiness, I sure like you more
now that you're no longer a bio-
morphic reserve
in the developmental leagues—nice cut,
but no turd in the parlor.

The enthusiast's dream is a rapt idol,
an escape module fashioned lika a second head
from government surplus neoprene.

Describe one bird you have never seen.
Show it to Happiness. Say, Happiness
these balloons are seized by razor wire
while yonder burgles a mortgaged wind.
We'll give you one chance to make it swing.

Taken from *The Case Against Happiness*

Duenna

TOM THOMPSON

A collar out of Fra Angelico   flickers across
the wall display—   modifiable bit by bit,

a cloaked form falls   to its knees in a room
in a far off city.   Is this a sexual film or a spiritual one

shadowing the wall?   It feels real under my finger-stubs,
humming.   By the window a spider-spindled ivy

is gowned in delicate dust,   extrudes patience from itself
leaf tip by leaf tip.   The greening tips sheathed in white

reach for a way out,   or in, through their own lit reflection.

Taken from *The Pitch*

House/Boat

JULIE CARR

Broad, the river belled in a thud of sun.

I climbed aboard, I rowed. A border flew open like a cough.
I leaned back to balance

my oars as they dipped
to green and red furrows of light.

My boat rocked, steady, un-steady.
Was I welcomed? It seemed I was as I gripped

and privately beheld.

The night soon lost its head.
Pulling up now, parking,

looking for something to eat,
to redeem.

The wind shook the seedpod but the seedpod
wasn't moved.

And though I thought I'd done the damage I was born for,

there was still so much to step through,
so much to mar.

Taken from *Equivocal*

Bird of Paradise

HENRIETTA GOODMAN

It's not a bird, and that's part
of the problem. It calls into question
what pleases the eye, makes you doubt

what you see. If paradise means
things are what they seem, there's no need

for a second glance, or a second guess.

You can take what you want
and what you want
will want to be taken. But this flower,

if that's what it is, has more to do
with possibility than with paradise,

more to do with iron burning
in slow motion, smoldering orange dust.

You're in a church and that's part
of the problem. Vows aren't supposed to be
made with crossed fingers,

but you keep thinking of how he showed you
the configuration of a V-8 engine—

palms out, fingers laced together,
the way you'd turn your hands
into a church for a child, and say the rhyme.

God as an engine seems right. Not God
to make promises to, or in front of,

but God to grind promises up,

burn them like gas. You know
they must be good for something,

that they aren't meant to only be kept.

Taken from *Take What You Want*

Body in Evidence

ANN KILLOUGH

She imagined the body in the exact middle of the evidence like a spider in its web.

Or perhaps like the prey still struggling incoherently over to one side of the web with the inward threads of the spider around it already seeming like its own unbearable guts.

*

Of course in her case the body turned out to be the body of the beloved idea of her nation.

Which seemed always of a different order than the fabric of ideological evidence, within which it hung like a lynched man.

Its main characteristic being intrusion, a helpless intrusive quality against which it turned out that the evidence had been organized all along and which was the only thing that remained incomprehensible.

Its main characteristic being a kind of mute surplus over all possible results to be obtained by its entrapment in the vast matrix of metaphors that she could now see stretching out on all sides infinitely.

The endlessly proliferating suburbs of entrepreneurial fabulist historical high-voltage gridlock sewage metaphoricity of the gluttonous national evangelism of understanding.

Within which the beloved idea hung like a lost sheep.

*

She was aware that her love for it was a naked thing.

Poor, universal.

She couldn't help it, it was all she had.

Taken from *Beloved Idea*

On Becoming Light

BILL RASMOVICZ

And there it was, the moth:
a child's hand wrestling itself in the grass.
Delirious, it fumbled its way out
from the black umbrella of a tree,
then landed on the stoop.

A frayed rope of light swung from the porch.
The moon was gorged on the dewy foment
of summer.

I set my hand near. It fluttered into my palm,
its weight no more than breath; its wings,
laments hammered into sheets of dust.

The world stalled on its axis, I could hear
the ocean in my bones, the night
nervous with cicadas from years ago.

It pulsed once toward the brightness:
impossible, that we must love what kills us.
I held my hand high to the light until it flew.

Taken from *The World in Place of Itself*

What if Christ Were a Snowflake Falling into the Sea?

DONALD REVELL

The water is taller than itself,
Covering spirits of the air beneath.
And so the land, so mountainous beside,
Does not exist.

Have you thought about the future?
Take your finger and rub it across a stone.
Do you feel it?
Heat where nothing but cold most certainly is.

The water does not suspect.
A distant star is plotting with the center of the Earth
Against the Earth.
And the lake rises. The outlet rivers rise.

There is also an uprising in Kiev.
God is love.

Taken from *A Thief of Strings*

Against Creation

DONALD REVELL

Sovereign of my heart, your temple
Is deep in the dead branches,
Moving only when the wind
Delves so far.

Eden is ago.
I mean, all's terror now.
Sovereign of my heart,
I am shouting at nightfall:
Bats above me,
Hummingbirds skittish below the bats,
Almost like dragonflies.

I am shouting into debris.
Immodest happiness in Eden's humility—
Ago.
Ago.

Adam's fall invented the future.
He tied the bats' wings onto dragonflies.
Nature, even as it dies, abhors imagination.
What men call Extinction,
I call Home.

Taken from *The Bitter Withy*

Once I was walking in the cold
and the light
kept leading, leaden
leading, leaden like a chant
for snow to come and knock out
school for another day.
I was talking with my friend
when my child interrupted.
With much effort he called me down
to fish the emptiness that would become
his brother from the river.

Taken from *King Baby*

You with a block of ice in your head,
a block in your stomach, a skirt of shells
and shells for eyes, leather ears,
wide mouth eliciting such tenderness,
face down in the stream
then carried through woods
by one (I will ever be your subject)
who took the long way home
through a grove of bamboo
and thawed your head body spine
in a bowl otherwise used for soup—
thus dissembled and known,
now can you rest?

Taken from *King Baby*

Furnace of Charity, Rose of Patience,
I never learned such formal appeal,
but here, will try:
Oh, roadside aster of emptiness,
hope of rot, a thing in need
of shelter too, oh, lion of ditchweed,
patient in ice, King of sudden
recognition, animal piss, crashpad of chance,
risen among gourds, dried, gutted and cut.
Sighted (dark irises of crimped shells) and given ears,
Baby found among the tangle, dried
and set upon a shelf, the crack in your head
lit in the early light of promise,
and again at nightfall, so that your white spine
carved and smoothed,
is a filament, scepter, sword conducting us all. . .

Taken from *King Baby*

It comes to me, amid all the abundance:
I almost passed you over.
I almost said *No, leave it there whatever
it is*—*brown bag of air, round, frozen
melon left from summer.*
I almost didn't dare.
Often I assemble myself
back at the beginning, beside
your simple promise:
if you pull me out, then. . .
It was not spoken. If it was,
I would have flown to it, I would have
been an eschatologist of the worst order,
reading groundswells, star charts, daybreak
for *then what, then what?*
I do not want to know the end,
your end, my end, oh, keep me from it
and from knowing what you promised
(though I think it's blooming).
Let me remember:
my son's arms couldn't reach
so I took over. I pulled you out
and held you dripping very close,
while everyone waited
to see what the air and light, just after a promise,
an old, old fable reconstituted, looked like.

Taken from *King Baby*

LIA PURPURA

King Baby, are you singing or asking to be fed?
Does need, like a pine tree, grow a knot at each limb's tip
and from there spring an arc of spikes—an explosion
held against the sky (the sky not blue, just white, this cold,
      late spring)
the needles conducting, the loose,
reticulate ends charged, alert, attentive—
such need! You sent yours out? Kept yours in?
I see into your mouth, cut wide like a ditch,
it's as dark as night fallen, or morning unrisen, I can't tell which,
but there, all the red's contained in black,
and back of the throat, I hear it decided: song, and not hunger.

Taken from *King Baby*

Insurance

for Jerry Waldor

My father and I,
salesmen ourselves,
said no to a man
selling roses.
The road, a whip
laid on the land.
Both quiet
after declining.
My father drives
I give directions.

Taken from *Door to a Noisy Room*

Handshake

PETER WALDOR

Very small is very beautiful
where the vein shakes
hands with the artery;
shake of strangers
who sense they want
to be friends.
Once, my father surprised
me by shaking my hand.
Once, he spilled a basket
of peaches into a stream.

Taken from *Door to a Noisy Room*

Jealous

FRANK GIAMPIETRO

Food meant nothing to Glenn Gould, he could go for hours
without thinking of it. Because of this, I suppose
I should like his music, but I just feel jealous.
I myself never engage
in anything food doesn't make better.
In fact, most of the time, I prefer just the food.
Wallace Stevens looks as though he was well-fed.
He was the vice president of an insurance company.
He said poetry *is simply the desire to contain*
the world wholly within one's own perception of it. I'm reminded
of my wife who made this most excellent fudge
and how she brought it to me with a cup of coffee
on a tray saying *chocolate dreams of coffee and coffee*
dreams of chocolate. Surely she has contained the world
by making it, and if not by making it, then by thinking
to bring me a piece of it with coffee on a tray.
She never writes down the ingredients;
she claims making food like this helps her
not eat it. And she just loves Glenn Gould.
Did I mention she can recite movies, scene
by scene? Sonny Rollins
could do the same thing with melodies: often he wouldn't
even need to hear endings to know them.
But that was a minor jealousy, and anyway,
doesn't a melody always end with the note on which it began?

Taken from *Begin Anywhere*

The Temple Gate Called Beautiful

David Kirby

Acts 3:2.

It says HELL IS HOT HOT HOT HOT
    and NO SEX WITH MEN ALOUD
and NO ICE WATER IN HELL
    on the hundreds of washers and dryers
        and air conditioner housings that stud
the land around outsider artist W.C. Rice's house in Prattville,
    though Mr. Rice isn't well today,

    so I'm chatting through the bedroom window
        of a man I visit every three-four years
to talk a while and then stroll the property
    that offers an ineluctable foreknowledge of The Pit
        to people like me, though Mr. Rice has always been
nice as pie, never proselytizing or even asking
    if I've been saved, which, according to him,

    either you are or you aren't. It's like day or night
        with W.C., sun or moon, fish or fowl. Beatles, Stones.
Montague, Capulet. Merchant copy, customer copy. Elvis, Frank:
    there's no Elvis *and* Frank in W.C.'s cosmology,
        no gray area at all, though we all want one, don't we,
we all want to be good, as George Orwell said,
    but not too good, and not all the time, and now

    Mr. Rice is telling me about the woman
        who came by at eleven the previous evening
after Mrs. Rice had already tacked up
    the cardboard sign that says it's too late to visit now
        but invites folks to return the next morning,
but the woman was crying so hard, and her teenaged daughter
    and her daughter's friend, too,

that they let her in, and it turned out her husband,
    who'd been physically abusive to her
their whole time together, had himself
    been beaten to death that very afternoon
        by a couple of these Pike County Paladins
who either had a strong sense of how
    the whole karma thing works or, more likely,

    were just repaying him in a familiar currency,
        only more of it, though the event had triggered
in his new widow not a feeling of gladness
    or simply relief but that peculiar remorse
        that overtakes us when somebody dies
that we just hated the shit out of in the first place,
    and now she was asking Mr. Rice if he could say

    where her husband was right now, this very minute,
        like, between this world and heaven, and, if so,
could she pray him up there, and you don't have to have
    a divinity degree from one of the area Bible colleges
        to guess that Mr. Rice's answer was a clear "Nope,"
a definite "He's pretty much where you saw him last,"
    and probably not even the "pretty much"!

And as Mr. Rice is going on about this concrete
    if somewhat unfeeling application of his belief system,
I'm thinking of how I was reading Andrew Motion's
    new Keats biography last night in room 246
        of the Fairfield Inn in nearby Montgomery
and came across a passage on Sir Astley Cooper,
    Keats' training surgeon at Guy's Hospital,

the same Sir Astley Cooper who said
    a surgeon must have "an eagle's eye,
a lady's hand, and a lion's heart," and at the same time,
    I thought, To what profession do these attributes
        not apply? And the answer is,
Mr. Rice's! When some audience members
    booed a drunk Jerry Lee Lewis one time,

he gestured toward the back of the hall
    and said, "Them doors swing both ways."
Not here on Highway 86 near Prattville, though,
    not on Mr. Rice's property. Doors only go one way here;
        you're either safe or out on Mr. Rice's
diamond. You're either kosher or treyf. It's Heaven or Hell for you,
    not to put too fine a point on it, and usually Hell.

But as the smart-alecks say, if you go to Hell
    for doing Satan's work up here, why would
he punish you when you got to his place? Some of Mr. Rice's work
    suggests that men in Hell are having sex
        with other men, but if that's what you like. . .
At the Montgomery Museum of Fine Arts
    are paintings by Sargent, Hopper, and Rothko

as well as the sculpture of another outsider artist,
    Charlie "Tin Man" Lucas, who makes animals
out of car parts. Nothing by Mr. Rice in that museum, though:
    the people in charge don't mind if a busload of tourists
        sees a deer made out of shock absorbers,
but they wouldn't want them to pause before a Sargent heiress
    with her silk habiliments and upswept tresses

and Grecian Urn-ish guarantees of immorality
    and then stumble over a rusty Kelvinator
on which someone has painted YOU WILL DIE in red house paint.
    No, the outskirts are right for Mr. Rice,
        not Art's well-appointed townhouse.
You leave Montgomery through the temple gate that leads from town
    to country, and on both sides, look: beautiful.

Taken from *The Temple Gate Called Beautiful*

The Origin

JANE MEAD

of what happened is not in language—
of this much I am certain.
Six degrees south, six east—

and you have it: the bird
with the blue feathers, the brown bird—
same white breasts, same scaly

ankles. The waves between us—
house light and transform motion
into the harboring of sounds in language.—

Where there is newsprint
the fact of desire is turned from again—
and again. Just the sense

that what remains might well be held up—
later, as an ending.
Twice I have walked through this life—

once for nothing, once
for facts: fairy-shrimp in the vernal pool—
glassy-winged sharpshooter

on the falling vines. Count me—
among the animals, their small
committed calls.—

Count me among
the living. My greatest desire—
to exist in a physical world.

Taken from *The Usable Field*

Trans-Generational Haunting

JANE MEAD

They come to you in dreams,
the dearly departed. They
come to you again and again—
elsewhere and otherwise included.

The same.

Then facing the purple mountain
and her shadow, I am watching
to keep them from slipping away.

I look inward—
I look outward—
all the same.

I was loved.
I was loved
and I return—

everywhere the dead
calling my name.

Taken from *The Usable Field*

To the Wren, No Difference No Difference to the Jay

JANE MEAD

I came a long
way to believe
in the blue jay

and I did not cheat
anyone. I
came a long way—

through complexities
of bird-sound and calendar
to believe in nothing

before I believed
in the jay.

Taken from *The Usable Field*

Aubade for Viña del Mar

IDRA NOVEY

I follow a stray dog
so he'll stop following me
and a violin begins forming
in the pocket of my coat.

I have no ear for tuning
but it is six a.m.
and I will soon be the owner
of a complete instrument.

Now it's almost seven o'clock
and a torso of wood
is pressing into my side.
In the other pocket, the poke
of a bow.

Taken from *The Next Country*

Meeting You, Age Four

KATHLEEN SHEEDER BONANNO

You have waved goodbye already,
we have waved already,
you have waved again until
there's nothing left
for us to do with dignity but go.

We back out of the lot
in one large economic swoop,
like a giant hand
has yanked us from behind.

You lift a sober little chin,
your face full upon us
as we pull away.

The funny sound
we need to fix begins
from under the inscrutable hood
of the old Maverick.
A tiny, tinny ball
riding a roulette wheel,
waiting to pick a number.

I do not need to look at David.
He does not need to look at me.
We drive straight home.
We look ahead.
The little ball whirrs:
We want you, we want you, we want you.

Taken from *Slamming Open the Door*

Death Barged In

KATHLEEN SHEEDER BONANNO

In his Russian greatcoat,
slamming open the door
with an unpardonable bang,
and he has been here ever since.

He changes everything,
rearranges the furniture,
his hand hovers
by the phone;
he will answer now, he says;
he will be the answer.

Tonight he sits down to dinner
at the head of the table
as we eat, mute;
later, he climbs into bed
between us.

Even as I sit here,
he stands behind me
clamping two
colossal hands on my shoulders
and bends down
and whispers to my neck:
From now on,
you write about me.

Taken from *Slamming Open the Door*

The New Realism

JOANNA FUHRMAN

It starts when you enter a body of water
named after a forgotten suburb, or when
you tiptoe to the edge of an apartment,
naked, carrying a single egg.

When the New Realism strikes,
you might find yourself listening
to soup evaporate like I did
after every other pleasure failed me

a million times. Try to drape yourself
in Edwardian post-punk glory.
Look into the mirror. Erase the idea
of what you thought of as self.

Andy Warhol's eyes are now your eyes.
Wear them until they break. Wear
them until they leak. Wear them until
they are your only eyes. Then lose them.

Finally, you will be as profound
as an air conditioner. You will be the negative
space between awkward teeth, the neon fluid
missing from every television sex scene.

Taken from *Pageant*

The Rabies Treatment

CAREY SALERNO

By the time we were all through,
every tool was laid out on the table.

Our arms so weak, we dropped all the papers;
thumping hearts wild to escape our chests.

But it was over and the body rolled
in a bundle tied up, slumped next to us.

For a long while, we gaped at the head
upside down on the table next to a line of dull tools.

We had scissored it off, trying each blade
finally breaking the bone with hedge cutters.

The head so still—even when I perched
its little neck on my knee,

coming undone, being sawed, twisted, vised
between two dull blades, the head didn't bulge an eye.

And we, sweaty-fingered, remarked how hard it was,
how thick the neck skin, how

there was hardly any blood, the table kept so clean
and the tools, too; none finished the job

entirely. We pulled with our hands. Yours on the body,
mine on the head. We yanked apart the tiny raccoon.

How it felt finally to break it, and how we each half-expected
the coon to come alive, hiss and claw its way free.

The tools we sluiced, head in a box,
headless body dumped behind the shelter

in a rusty casket. The open neck.
Our hands already washed.

Taken from *Shelter*

Unraveling

CAREY SALERNO

That we never parted ways, never
untied the last breath. I couldn't stop

cowering below the wolf. Always looked
back over my shoulder, saw the dark stalker there.

Long ivory legs rose to darkness. In sleep
she hung like hot breath over my neck,

my racing artery, bloody nails printed
the bedclothes, the stench of thick undercoat.

I come undone all over again.
Her limp tongue never left me. She knew

how we would be, dug a grave in my body.
Now we are always alone.

I fear coming close to it, dance before it
awkwardly, not wanting to stain our white ribbon,

lampblack breaking the headstone.

Taken from *Shelter*

The Sound of My Mother Crying

Reginald Dwayne Betts

The first step to confessing is to walk into a parking
lot with a pistol. A .380 because it disappears in your palm
like loaded dice. There were strands of a song cupped
in my hands that night & I want to remember.
The man before me wore a white shirt he'd worn
too many times. The light was jail cell light & reflected
a morning I wish hadn't awakened me. Parole
had been dumped for truth in sentencing & GM
had laid off half the people in a city I've never visited.
There is a secret in all of this & so everything I denied
could still be denied, taken back. A head fake, if you will.
The tape recorder spoke to me, read back my words. But
listen, the man in his car wasn't as much asleep as
waiting for something in his life to happen. To move
him from where he was to where he could go &
there are people I know who have died waiting to be.
I opened his hurt. I pushed the eye of the gun under
his ear & thought of what angle his shock against
my fear formed. I taunted him, maybe. Asked if he
was a cop. There is a song, "Life Goes On," that ends
in a life sentence. Imagine this: I scribbled
my name on the confession. You tell your mother that.
Tell her you admitted that the gun was
a kiss & it was so close to the forehead of the sleeping
man that if you were his woman he would have moaned.

Taken from *Shahid Reads His Own Palm*

Shahid Reads His Own Palm

REGINALD DWAYNE BETTS

I come from the cracked hands of men who used
    the smoldering ends of blunts to blow shotguns,

men who arranged their lives around the mystery
    of the moon breaking a street corner in half.

I come from "Swann Road" written in a child's
    slanted block letters across a playground fence,

the orange globe with black stripes in Bishop's left
    hand, untethered and rolling to the sideline,

a crowd openmouthed, waiting to see the end
    of the sweetest crossover in a Virginia state pen.

I come from Friday night's humid and musty air,
    Junk Yard Band cranking in a stolen Bonneville,

a tilted bottle of Wild Irish Rose against my lips
    and King Hedley's secret written in the lines of my palm.

I come from beneath a cloud of white smoke, a lit pipe
    and the way glass heats rocks into a piece of heaven,

from the weight of nothing in my palm,
    a bullet in an unfired snub-nosed revolver.

And every day the small muscles in my finger threaten to pull
    a trigger, slight and curved like my woman's eyelashes.

Taken from *Shahid Reads His Own Palm*

Cesarean

NICOLE COOLEY

Now the irises rage light   spiked tongues
at the hospital window

How I would like to just unravel

Through glass   cut leaves curl like fingers
in my throat

I once wished to take myself apart

There is no space between us   body caught in my body

There is the voice telling me *there are many ways
to give birth*

The lesson chalked on the sidewalk,
these lines are surgeon sketches—

to save her   cut here and here and here

Taken from *Milk Dress*

Accounting for the Wren, the Rocket, and the Immaterial

DANIEL JOHNSON

The sky becomes what is added to it—
       a radio tower, stratus clouds, one hundred Chinese kites,

until one day, a day like today when winds gust east, then
       west, blowing hard off the lake,

the sky becomes what is taken away—

       a vapor trail vanished: the absence of geese: a gaping
       space where before there was none.

Begin again the slow math of loss. Use feathers, flint,
       a scattering of seeds,

until the sky, once more, fills with that which is offered to it—

       our love-cries and curses, our Kaddishes, our longing
and singing, our long, long keening.

Taken from *How to Catch a Falling Knife*

Quince

MIHAELA MOSCALIUC

is what I think of when you ask for truth.
Vilvam, Cydonia oblongata, Cydonia vulgaris I prefer,
though *melimelum, strythion, quitte* hold
the musky pubescence in just the right calyx of sounds.

Golden apple, sparrow apple, must apple—
whose joke, this mistranslation
forever hatching in the paws of Pompeii's bears,
parting Eve's lips, lifting Aphrodite's palm,
trading mortal praise for eternal lust and blood?

Quince stoning the bride's chariot,
                showering the nuptial bed,
pomander spicing crisp winters,
                warding off evil like a cloven voodoo doll,
peltea shelving desire, shining like jarred amber,
                enjambing the pantry's delights,
tattoo pivoting the contortionist's body on a Dominican beach,
                do you recognize me?
Joan of Arc entering Orleans, 1429, to liberate the French from the English,
                honored with the gift of *cotignac*.
March 16, 1629, Massachusetts Bay Colony's memorandum:
                "Send quince seeds."

Apples: so amiable, utterly pliable, fond of mutation, eager to please.
Quince:
        stay with me stay with me deep into winter

Taken from *Father Dirt*

The Piano Teacher

CHAD SWEENEY

A music box wound too tightly will explode,
playing its song all at once.
The practice is to unwind the song slowly.
Think of this when you touch the key of C.

A black hole warbles the note B-flat
in waves as wide as galaxies
forty octaves below your house.
Think of this when you love someone.

Sound has its own horizon.
Our meetings will happen there.
The cello is floating away.
The ribs of a tiger are rippling.

Taken from *Parable of Hide and Seek*

lie down too

L E S L E L E W I S

Only you are standing in the standing house.

You can't believe your sick insides don't show.

You take different slowdown pills.

The ocean in bed is calm and you will go there.

Four times now, you've been made younger with wanting to.

You dream you take a sleeping pill and sleep.

You look through the holiday ham to the bone and have visions.

It is sunny and flat and perfect.

Cows lie in the snow in the air direct from Labrador.

The sheep and the chair and the house lie down too.

Taken from *lie down too*

Self-portrait as Thousandfurs

Stacy Gnall

To have been age enough.
To have been leg enough.
Been enough bold. Said no.
Been a girl drown into that
negative construction. Or said yes
on condition of a dress. To be yours
if my skirts skimmed the floors.
To have demanded each seam
celestial, appealed for planetary pleats.

　　　　And when you saw the sun a sequin,
the moon a button shaped from glass,
and in the stars a pattern
for a dress, when the commission
proved too minute, and the frocks
hung before me like hosts,
to have stood then at the edge
of the wood, heard a hound's bark
and my heart hark in return.

　　　　To have seen asylum in the scruffs
of neck—mink, lynx, ocelot, fox,
Kodiak, ermine, wolf—felt a claw
curve over my sorrow then. Said yes
on condition of a dress. To be yours
if my skirts skimmed the floors.
To have demanded each seam
just short of breathing, my mouth
a-beg for bestial pleats.

　　　　And when you saw tails as tassels,
underskins sateen, and in entrails
damasks of flowers and fruit,
when the bet proved not too broad
for you, and before me, the clock held

open as a boast, to have slipped
into that primitive skin. To have
turned my *how how* into a howl. To have
picked up my heavy hem and run.

Taken from *Heart First into the Forest*

Miss Sally on the *Grandmother Fires*

SHARA MCCALLUM

Hear what I tell yu: God promised Noah,
No more water. The fire next time.
That evening, mi sit down on the verandah
teking in a lickle fresh air when news reach
of the women dead in them sleep.
Lickle by lickle, the rest of the story come out:
two young boys acting like men, like God himself.
153 dead—and fi what? Fi win election?

Mi dear, in all mi years I never imagine
is so low we would stoop.
For a people who know
what it is to be the lamb,
how we go lead our own
to slaughter?

Taken from *This Strange Land*

Psalm for Kingston

SHARA MCCALLUM

If I forget thee, O Jerusalem

—PSALM 137

City of Jack Mandora—*mi nuh choose none*—of Anancy
    prevailing over Mongoose, Breda Rat, Puss, and Dog, Anancy
        saved by his wits in the midst of chaos and against all odds;
    of bawdy Big Boy stories told by peacock-strutting boys, *hush-hush*
but loud enough to be heard by anyone passing by the yard.

City of market women at Half-Way-Tree with baskets
    atop their heads or planted in front of their laps, squatting or standing
        with arms akimbo, *susuing* with one another, clucking
    their tongues, calling in voices of pure sugar, *come dou-dou: see
the pretty bag I have for you,* then kissing their teeth when you saunter off.

City of school children in uniforms playing dandy shandy
    and brown girl in the ring—*tra-la-la-la-la*—
        eating bun and cheese and bulla and mangoes,
    juice sticky and running down their chins, bodies arced
in laughter, mouths agape, heads thrown back.

City of old men with rheumy eyes, crouched in doorways,
    on verandahs, paring knives in hand, carving wood pipes
        or peeling sugar cane, of younger men pushing carts
    of roasted peanuts and oranges, calling out as they walk the streets
and night draws near, of coconut vendors with machetes in hand.

City where power cuts left everyone in sudden dark,
    where the kerosene lamp's blue flame wavered on kitchen walls,
        where empty bellies could not be filled,
    where *no eggs, no milk, no beef today* echoed
in shantytowns, around corners, down alleyways.

City where Marley sang, *Jah would never give the power to a baldhead*
      while baldheads reigned, where my parents chanted
            down Babylon—*Fire! Burn! Jah! Rastafari! Selassie I!*—
      where they paid weekly dues, saving for our passages back to Africa,
while in their beds my grandparents slept fitfully, dreaming of America.

City that lives under a long-memoried sun,
      where the gunmen of my childhood have been replaced
            by dons that rule neighbourhoods as fiefdoms, where violence
      and beauty still lie down together. City of my birth—
if I forget thee, who will I be, singing the Lord's song in this strange land?

Taken from *This Strange Land*

Ecstatic Vision

JANINE OSHIRO

The sound she made me make, it was
a what-
aphant. My voice

woke me to a girl
standing beside me.
She came to find and found what
in the room I could not see.
But the bed was bigger than I recalled
and the thing keeping
down my chest would not
let go. *Let me go.*

She would not let up
her stare.

Her hair was cut just
below her chin. She stood in
the bathroom's light
and stared at it

on top of me, a
whataphant awaking.

Taken from *Pier*

The Inadequacy of Pink

L a u r a   M c C u l l o u g h

The child lies with a towel beneath her.
The hibiscus splattered across her bathing suit
is the false color of innocence,
like the myth of tropical islands,
the imagined bartering of small shells for metal.

Pink is the color
of some tongues,
the inside of a conch,
a spot on someone's thigh after a scab has fallen off,

or the corners of a lifeguard's eyes.

After a long night away from the pool
on the beach at Sea Isle,
he imagines the new world
rising out of his lap,
remembering his last save,
a girl gone too deep
and the tube she'd slipped through—
how he'd waited for a crowd to gather around him,

but how they didn't,
not even the child's family,
who simply collected their towels and toys
and went home to make lunch
and go on with their day
as if nothing remarkable
had happened at all.

Taken from *Panic*

~~Eunice Waymon~~

MONICA A. HAND

my name an omen
my name sin

my name
my name a moan

Nina
Nina Simone

Taken from *me and Nina*

Tea Palinode (18th & Sanchez)

STEPHEN MOTIKA

In removing sidewalks from San Francisco, I planted trees, oaks and laurel.
An arc by bay, I sat in parallel time, scratching the Velcro clasp of revealing
and not revealing. Having made amends in a small space, we stepped lakeside,
fostered beads and tears. The mist of God fell away, the paralysis instilled;
I walked alone, books on fern morphology in hand, until the region of lawns
unrolled. Tending to death, this untouched shade, we troubled, uncoupled.
Lost to sweep of Queen Anne's lace and leaflets, our errant grip slips, slack.
Wrapped in English, sleep exhumed a theory at map's edge, cast in ornament,
artifice, my tongue an observer.

Taken from *Western Practice*

Beneath the Arctic Floe

MATTHEW PENNOCK

This shrewd quotient,
spiraling and ridged like the fractal
geometry of a seahorse tail.

My new obsessions: electoral math,
Greenland sharks,
the doctrine of duck and cover.

Portrait of a symptom on the couch:

Sleeper, we are blind
and sometimes
eat our own.

The bed, too empty.

Sleeper, do not fear.
If you are buried with mortar and brick,
you have become too heavy.

Buildings do not collapse
due to fire or some
architect's mistake.

They grow tired simply—
our asking them to hold us.

Taken from *Sudden Dog*

Small Cosmos

JANE SPRINGER

I've seen a wheat field riven where an almighty finger of wind flicked a silo into
the green sky like it was an aluminum flea vaulted towards oblivion—

grain showered the ant & shrew alike & in the wake of disaster—even the
    gopher
turtle shook the dirt off her nose, to eat.

Should I love a ruined family of giants more than I love the unasked-for blessing
befallen to the smallest creatures?

(To see a thing riven is to wish I'd given you one brass button for luck.)

I've heard a river waltz through laced hands of the levee toward a grand new
partnering of earth & water—

then stood for weeks in the tenebrous waters of that breaking, wondering,

                        would my own feet ever dry enough for dancing?

Men with shirts tied round their waists waded over highways with buckets &
plunged makeshift spears into flashing fish—were they poor men?

It makes no sense to speak of the poverty & riches of love. Love,

come as a cloud & I will stay in the country below you. If you are, by night,
a fire, I will follow your fragrance of ashes into the wilderness.

I will eat your cornbread, pomegranate & fig. I will put away my ghosts & move
into whatever stone house you provide—

even if it means learning a new way of speaking. Out of hammered silver, I send
two trumpets with which you may call me.

Taken from *Murder Ballad*

ABOUT THE CONTRIBUTORS

ALICE JAMES Books *has made every effort to collect complete biographical information from our contributors. Bios marked with an asterisk were crafted on behalf of the contributor by Alice James Books. For more information on our poets, please visit www.alicejamesbooks.org.*

CATHERINE ANDERSON is the author of *In the Mother Tongue* (Alice James Books) and *The Work of Hands* (Perugia Press). Her poems have appeared in *The Southern Review, Harvard Review, Prairie Schooner, Many Mountains Moving*, and many other journals. In 2010, she won the Richard Peterson Poetry Prize sponsored by the *Crab Orchard Review*. She is an advocate for limited-English speakers in Kansas City, Missouri.

DOUG ANDERSON has poems forthcoming in *The Massachusetts Review, Cutthroat, Cimarron Review, San Pedro River Review, Raleigh Review, Badlands*, and *Verdad*. His last book, *Keep Your Head Down*, a memoir, was published in 2009 by W.W. Norton. He is a Visiting Assistant Professor of Poetry at the University of Massachusetts Amherst.

KATHLEEN AGUERO's poetry collections include *Investigations: The Mystery of the Girl Sleuth, Daughter Of, The Real Weather*, and *Thirsty Day*. She has also co-edited three volumes of multicultural literature for the University of Georgia Press and is poetry editor of *Solstice Literary Magazine*. She teaches at Pine Manor College in Chestnut Hill, Massachusetts in both the undergraduate and low-residency MFA programs and in Changing Lives through Literature, an alternative sentencing program.

CATHERINE BARNETT is the recipient of a Guggenheim Fellowship, a Whiting Writers' Award, and a Pushcart Prize. Her first book of poems, *Into Perfect Spheres Such Holes Are Pierced*, was published in 2004 by Alice James Books. Her second poetry collection, *The Game of Boxes*, is forthcoming from Graywolf Press in August 2012. She teaches at Barnard, The New School, and NYU, works as an independent editor, and is running the 2012 Emerging Poets Residency at Poets House.

DAN BEACHY-QUICK is the author of five books of poetry, including *North True South Bright* and *Circle's Apprentice*, as well as two collaborative collections, *Conversities* (with poet Srikanth Reddy) and *Work from Memory* (with Matthew Goulish). He is also the author of two prose collections, *A Whaler's Dictionary* and *Wonderful Investigations*. He teaches in the MFA Program at Colorado State University.

ROBIN BECKER, Liberal Arts Research Professor of English and Women's Studies at The Pennsylvannia State University, has received fellowships from the Massachusetts Cultural Council, the National Endowment for the Arts, and the Bunting Institute at Harvard. Her published collections in the Pitt Poetry Series include *Giacometti's Dog*, *All-American Girl*, *The Horse Fair*, and *Domain of Perfect Affection*. Becker serves as contributing and poetry editor for the *Women's Review of Books* where her column "Field Notes" appears regularly. During the 2010-2011 academic year, Becker served as the Penn State Laureate.

SUZANNE E. BERGER'S first book, *These Rooms*, was published by Penmaen Press; her second, *Legacies*, was published by Alice James Books. *Horizontal Woman*, a memoir, was published by Houghton Mifflin. She teaches an advanced poetry seminar at Lesley University, and has had residencies at The MacDowell Colony and the Virginia Center for the Arts. A Pushcart Prize has come her way as well as a place on the New Hampshire Council for the Arts. Presently she is working on a novel and another collection of poetry.

REGINALD DWAYNE BETTS is a husband and father of two young sons. As a poet, essayist, and national spokesperson for the Campaign for Youth

Justice, Betts writes and lectures about the impact of mass incarceration on American society. In 2011 Betts was awarded a Radcliffe Fellowship to Harvard University's Radcliffe Institute of Advanced Studies. The author of the memoir, *A Question of Freedom* (Avery/Penguin, 2009) and the collection of poetry, *Shahid Reads His Own Palm* (Alice James Books, 2010), Betts' work possesses a careful, complicated, and often difficult-to-confront intimacy that challenges conventional ideas about crime, masculinity, and redemption. In 2010 he was awarded an NAACP Image Award for *A Question of Freedom*, and a Soros Justice Fellowship to complete *The Circumference of a Prison*, a work of nonfiction exploring the criminal justice system's role in the everyday lives of Americans who have not committed crimes.

KATHLEEN SHEEDER BONANNO is the director of Musehouse. Her book, *Slamming Open the Door*, was among the top ten best-selling books of poetry in America in 2009. Bonanno was interviewed on NPR's Fresh Air with Terry Gross and has had her book favorably reviewed in *The New York Times*. In 2008, she was awarded a Women of Courage/Women of Inspiration Award by Lutheran Settlement House for her anti-violence advocacy.

CAROLE A. BORGES spent most of her childhood aboard an old schooner on the Mississippi River. She learned the art of storytelling from fishermen, the people who lived along riverbanks, and also from the river itself. Her poems have appeared in *Poetry* and numerous other literary magazines. Her essays and newspaper articles were published in *City View*, *Eva*, *Pacific Yachting*, and *Rudder Magazine*. She currently lives in North Knoxville, Tennessee.

JULIE CARR is the author of four books of poetry, most recently *100 Notes on Violence* (winner of the Sawtooth Poetry Prize) and *Sarah—Of Fragments and Lines* (a National Poetry Series selection). *Equivocal* came out from Alice James Books in 2007. *Surface Tension: Ruptural Time and the Poetics of Desire* is out from Dalkey Archive in 2012. She is the co-publisher, with Tim Roberts, of Counterpath Press. She lives in Denver and teaches at the University of Colorado in Boulder.

NICOLE COOLEY grew up in New Orleans and is the author of four books of poems, including *Milk Dress* (Alice James Books, 2010), and a novel. She directs the MFA Program in Creative Writing and Literary Translation at Queens College-City University of New York. She lives outside of New York City with her husband and her two daughters.

ROBERT CORDING teaches English and creative writing at College of the Holy Cross where he is the Barrett Professor of Creative Writing. He has published six collections of poems: *Life-list*, which won the Ohio State University Press/Journal Award in 1987; *What Binds Us To This World* (Copper Beech Press, 1991); *Heavy Grace* (Alice James Books, 1996); *Against Consolation* (CavanKerry Press, 2002); *Common Life*, (CavanKerry Press, 2006); and his newest, *Walking With Ruskin* (CavanKerry Press, 2010). He has received two National Endowment for the Arts Fellowships in poetry and two poetry grants from the Connecticut Commission of the Arts. His poems have appeared in numerous publications, such as *The Nation, Georgia Review, The Southern Review, Poetry, Kenyon Review, New England Review, Orion,* and *The New Yorker.*

CYNTHIA CRUZ is the author of *Ruin* (Alice James Books) and *The Glimmering Room* (Four Way Books.) She is the recipient of fellowships from Yaddo, The MacDowell Colony, and a Hodder Fellowship from Princeton. Her poems have been published in *The New Yorker, Paris Review, Boston Review, The American Poetry Review,* and *Kenyon Review* among other journals and included in *Isn't it Romantic: 100 Love Poems by Younger American Poets* and *The Iowa Anthology of New American Poetries.* She lives in Brooklyn.

PATRICIA CUMMING and her husband, Edward Cumming, graduated from Harvard in 1954. He died in 1960. They had two daughters. Starting in 1962, she and others founded The Theatre Company of Boston, the Writing Program at MIT, and Alice James Books. She has taught writing at Harvard University, Bard College, Sarah Lawrence College, the University of Massachusetts Boston, and the University of Massachusetts Dartmouth. She continues to publish poems (most recently in *Calyx*), and is now collecting them. She and Lee Rudolph ended their engagement and married in 2007.

CHRISTINA DAVIS is the author of *An Ethic* (Nightboat Books, 2013) and *Forth A Raven* (Alice James Books, 2006). Her poems have appeared in *The American Poetry Review, jubilat, Pleiades, Paris Review*, and other publications. A graduate of the University of Pennsylvania and Oxford University, she is the recipient of the Witter Bynner Award from the Library of Congress, selected by U.S. Poet Laureate Kay Ryan, and currently serves as curator of the Woodberry Poetry Room at Harvard University.

DEBORAH DENICOLA is the author of six collections of poetry, most recently, *Original Human* (World Tech, 2010), and her memoir, *The Future That Brought Her Here* (Nicholas Hays/Ibis Press, 2009). She is a freelance editor and also practices Dream Image Work. She received the Santa Barbara Poetry Award, 2008 and The Paul Hoover Critical Essay Award from *Packingtown Review,* 2009 and has received an artist's fellowship from the National Endowment for the Arts. Her web site is www.intuitivegateways.com.

THEODORE DEPPE grew up in Indiana and has lived in Ireland since 2000. He worked as an RN for twenty years, and has taught poetry in MFA programs in Ireland, England, and the U.S. He coordinates Stonecoast in Ireland for the Stonecoast MFA program in Maine. His work has received two fellowships from the National Endowment for the Arts and a Pushcart Prize. Salmon Poetry in Ireland published *Cape Clear: New and Selected Poems* in 2002, and Tupelo published *Orpheus on the Red Line* in 2009.

XUE DI was born in Beijing. He is the author of three volumes of collected works and one book of criticism on contemporary Chinese poetry in Chinese. In English translation, he has published four full-length books and four chapbooks. His work has appeared in numerous American journals and anthologies and has been translated into several languages. Xue Di is a two-time recipient of the Hellman-Hammett Award, and a recipient of the Lannan Foundation Fellowship.

JEANNINE DOBBS has a PhD from the University of New Hampshire, and she has taught writing and English as a second language there and elsewhere. Her poetry has appeared in numerous journals, and she was a 2008 nominee for a Pushcart Prize.

AMY DRYANSKY'S first book, *How I Got Lost So Close to Home*, was published by Alice James Books and individual poems have appeared in a variety of anthologies and journals, including *Orion, New England Review, Harvard Review,* and *make/shift*. She's been nominated for several Pushcart Prizes and awarded fellowships to The MacDowell Colony, Vermont Studio Center, Villa Montalvo, and the Bread Loaf Writers' Conference. She's also a former associate at the Five College Women's Studies Research Center at Mt. Holyoke College, where she looked at the impact of motherhood on the work of women poets. She currently works for a regional land trust, teaches in the Writing Program at Hampshire College and writes about what it's like to navigate the territory of mother/artist/poet at her blog, *Pokey Mama*. Her second book, *Grass Whistle*, is forthcoming from Salmon Poetry.

JOCELYN EMERSON received the Robert Winner Memorial Award from the Poetry Society of America and is the author of *Sea Gate* (Alice James Books, 2002) as well as a chapbook, *Confirmations of the Rapt*.

B.H. FAIRCHILD'S *The Art of the Lathe* was a finalist for the National Book Award and received the William Carlos Williams Award, the Kingsley Tufts Poetry Award, the California Book Award, the PEN Center USA West Poetry Award, and the Natalie Ornish Poetry Award. He is the author of six books of poetry—including *Usher*, his most recent—and recipient of Guggenheim, Rockefeller (Bellagio), and National Endowment for the Arts fellowships.

MARJORIE FLETCHER is a co-founder of Alice James Books and served as president of the press for nearly twenty years.

JOANNA FUHRMAN is the author of four books of poetry: *Pageant* (Alice James Books, 2009), *Moraine* (Hanging Loose Press, 2006), *Ugh Ugh Ocean* (Hanging Loose Press, 2003), and *Freud in Brooklyn* (Hanging Loose Press, 2000). In 2011, Least Weasel published her chapbook, *The Emotive Function*. For more information visit: joannafuhrman.com.

ALLISON FUNK is the author of four books of poems: *The Tumbling Box, The Knot Garden, Living at the Epicenter,* and *Forms of Conversion.* Her work is collected in a number of anthologies, including *When She Named Fire: An Anthology of Contemporary Poetry by American Women* and *The Best American Poetry.* She is the recipient of awards from the National Endowment for the Arts, the Poetry Society of America, and *Poetry.* She is a Distinguished Professor of English at Southern Illinois University Edwardsville.

Since publishing her first book with Alice James Books, ERICA FUNKHOUSER has published four more books of poetry with Houghton Mifflin Harcourt. Her work has also appeared in numerous anthologies and magazines. She teaches the Advanced Poetry Writing Workshop at MIT and lives in Essex, Massachusetts.

RITA GABIS is a poet and prose writer whose work has appeared in *Harvard Review, Poetry,* and elsewhere. She is the recipient of a New York Foundation for the Arts grant for nonfiction as well as a poetry residency at the Provincetown Fine Arts Work Center. She is currently at work on a memoir for Bloomsbury. She lives and teaches in New York City.

ERIC GAMALINDA won the Asian American Literary Prize for *Zero Gravity,* and was recently shortlisted for the Man Asian Literary Prize. His collection of short stories, *People Are Strange,* was recently published by Black Lawrence Press. A multi-venue exhibit of "QRoems" (poems encrypted as QR codes) was part of the Asian American Arts Alliance's "Locating the Sacred" arts festival in 2012. He currently teaches at the Center for the Study of Ethnicity and Race at Columbia University.

SARAH GAMBITO is the author of the poetry collections *Delivered* (Persea Books) and *Matadora* (Alice James Books). She is Assistant Professor of English and Director of Creative Writing at Fordham University. Together with Joseph O. Legaspi, she co-founded Kundiman, a nonprofit organization serving Asian American poets.

FORREST GANDER'S most recent titles are *Core Samples from the World,* a NBCC Finalist, and *Redstart: An Ecological Poetics* (with John Kinsella). His most recent translation is *Watchword* by Villaurrutia Award-winning Mexican poet Pura Lopez Colome.

FRANK X. GASPAR holds an MFA from the Graduate Writing Program at University of California Irvine and is the author of five collections of poetry and two novels. Among his many fiction awards are a Barnes and Noble Discovery Award and the California Book Award for first fiction (novel, *Leaving Pico*) and a MassBook of the Year Award (novel, *Stealing Fatima*). In poetry he received multiple inclusions in *Best American Poetry,* four Pushcart Prizes, a National Endowment for the Arts Fellowship in Literature, and a California Arts Council Fellowship in Poetry. His first three collections have won the Morse, Anhinga, and Brittingham Prizes, and his fourth, *Night of a Thousand Blossoms* (Alice James Books), was listed by *Library Journal* as one of the twelve best books of poetry for 2004. He most recently held the Helio and Amelia Pedrosa/Luso-American Foundation Endowed Chair in Portuguese Studies at the University of Massachusetts Dartmouth. A new collection of poems, *Late Rapturous,* was published by Autumn House in 2012. He is currently teaching in Pacific University's MFA program and at work on a new novel.

KINERETH GENSLER (1922-2005) grew up in Chicago and Jerusalem. She received her BA from the University of Chicago and her MA from Columbia University. She married Walter Gensler, a professor of chemistry, settled in Belmont, Massachusetts, and had three children, Orin (Addis Ababa, Ethiopia), Daniel (Hyde Park, New York) and Gail (Seattle, Washington). At age 42, she returned to her childhood love of poetry and taught, wrote, and published for the next forty years. She participated in poetry groups in Boston and in Jerusalem, where she went every summer to visit her parents, sisters, and friends. Alice James Books and the Radcliffe Seminars were her professional homes.

FRANK GIAMPIETRO is the author of *Begin Anywhere* (Alice James Books, 2008) and creator of the online poetry projects La Fovea and Poems by

Heart. His writing has appeared in journals including *32 Poems*, *American Book Review*, *Barrow Street*, *Black Warrior Review*, *Cimarron Review*, *FENCE*, *Hayden's Ferry*, *Narrative*, *Ploughshares*, *Poetry Daily*, and *Rain Taxi*. Awards for his writing include fellowships from Virginia Center for the Creative Arts and Sewanee Writers' Conference. He earned his PhD in English from Florida State University and was a 2010-2012 resident scholar at *The Southern Review*.

*CELIA GILBERT is the author of five books of poetry: *An Ark of Sorts*, winner of the first Jane Kenyon Chapbook Award and *Bonfire* (both published by Alice James Books), *Queen of Darkness* (Viking Press), *Something to Exchange* (BlazeVOX Books), and an edition of new and selected poems in Polish and English published in Poland. Gilbert received a BA from Smith College and an MA from Boston University. She is also a printmaker and painter.

STACY GNALL is the author of *Heart First into the Forest*. She earned her undergraduate degree at Sarah Lawrence College and her MFA at the University of Alabama, and she is currently pursuing her PhD in Literature and Creative Writing at the University of Southern California. Her work has previously appeared in *The Cincinnati Review*, *The Florida Review*, *The Gettysburg Review*, *Indiana Review*, *The Laurel Review*, *The Spoon River Poetry Review*, and *Prairie Schooner*. Originally from Cleveland, Ohio she now lives in Los Angeles.

KEVIN GOODAN is the author of three books of poetry, most recently *Upper Level Disturbances* (Colorado State University/Center for Literary Publishing). He is Assistant Professor at Lewis-Clark State College and divides his time between Idaho, Montana, and Cape Cod.

HENRIETTA GOODMAN grew up in North Carolina and earned an MFA from the University of Montana and a PhD in English from Texas Tech University. Her first book of poetry, titled *Take What You Want*, won Alice James Books' 2006 Beatrice Hawley Award. Her poems have appeared in such journals as *The Massachusetts Review* and *New England Review*, and she has received the Boyden Wilderness Writing Residency, a fellowship from the Montana Arts Council, and other awards.

MIRIAM GOODMAN (1938-2008), beloved mother and poet, published two collections of poetry with Alice James Books, *Permanent Wave* (1977) and *Signal::Noise* (1982). She published a third collection, *Commercial Traveler*, with the Garden Street Press in 1996. From the early 1970s to the early 1980s, Miriam worked with the Alice James Books Poetry Cooperative when it was based in Cambridge, Massachusetts. She was a skilled and dedicated photographer. Though she passed away in 2008 after a brave battle with metastatic melanoma, Miriam's memorial exhibit "After a Certain Age" can currently be found at the Griffin Museum of Photography for anyone who wishes to remember her considerable contributions to the creative world.

JEFFREY GREENE is the author of four collections of poetry, a memoir, and two personalized nature books. He received the Morse Prize, the Jarrell Prize, and the "Discovery"/*The Nation* Award, and his work has been supported by fellowships from the National Endowment for the Arts, the Connecticut Commission on the Arts, and Humanities Texas. He is an Associate Professor at the American University of Paris and teaches for the Pan-European Low-Residency MFA Program.

JOAN JOFFE HALL learned to read at age four while her mother's back was turned. After further education at Vassar College and Stanford University, she taught for forty years, mostly at University of Connecticut, in English and Women's Studies. She has published *The Rift Zone* (W. C. Williams Prize finalist), Alice James Books' *Romance & Capitalism at the Movies* (Pulitzer nominee), *In Angled Light*, and a volume of stories, *Summer Heat*. Her fiction, memoirs, and poetry have appeared widely in journals and chapbooks.

FORREST HAMER is the author of *Call & Response* (Alice James Books, 1995), winner of the Beatrice Hawley Award; *Middle Ear* (Roundhouse, 2000), winner of the Northern California Book Award; and *Rift* (Four Way Books, 2007). His work is widely anthologized, and appears in three editions of *The Best American Poetry*. He has received fellowships from the California Arts Council and the Bread Loaf Writers' Conference, and he has taught on the poetry faculty of the Callaloo Creative Writing Workshops.

MONICA A. HAND, author of *me and Nina* (Alice James Books, 2012), is also a book artist. Her poems have appeared in numerous publications including *Aunt Chloe, Black Renaissance Noire, Naugatuck River Review, The Sow's Ear, Drunken Boat, Beyond the Frontier, African-American Poetry for the 21st Century*, and *Gathering Ground: A Reader Celebrating Cave Canem's First Decade and American Creative Writers on Class*. She has an MFA in Poetry and Poetry-in-Translation from Drew University and currently is a PhD candidate in Creative Writing at the University of Missouri-Columbia. She is a fellow of Cave Canem, a home for the many voices of African American poetry; and, a founding member of Poets for Ayiti, a diverse collective of poets committed to the power of poetry to transform and to educate.

MARIE HARRIS' books of poetry include *Weasel in the Turkey Pen* and *Your Sun, Manny: A Prose Poem Memoir*. She is the author of three children's books, including *G is for Granite* and *The Girl Who Heard Colors* (Penguin, 2013). She is working on several projects about the life and work of Amy Beach, America's first female composer. For more information visit, www.marieharris.com.

MATTHEA HARVEY is the author of four books of poetry (*Of Lamb, Modern Life, Sad Little Breathing Machine*, and *Pity the Bathtub Its Forced Embrace of the Human Form*) and two books for children, *The Little General and the Giant Snowflake* and *Cecil the Pet Glacier*.

*BEATRICE HAWLEY (1944-1985) taught at Brandeis University and first published with the encouragement of Denise Levertov. In addition to *Making the House Fall Down*, her first book, Hawley published one other, *Nothing Is Lost* (Apple-Wood Press, 1979). *The Collected Poems of Beatrice Hawley* (Zoland Books, 1989) was edited by Denise Levertov and published posthumously.

*FANNY HOWE is the author of more than twenty books of poetry and prose. Her recent collections of poetry include *The Lyrics* (Graywolf Press, 2007), *On the Ground* (2004), *Gone* (2003), *Selected Poems* (2000), and *Forged* (1999). She is also the author of several novels and prose collections, including, *The Winter Sun: Notes on a Vocation* (Graywolf Press, 2009) and *The Lives of a Spirit / Glasstown: Where Something Got Broken* (Nightboat Books, 2005). Howe has taught at MIT, Tufts University, and at the University of California at San Diego among other places.

CYNTHIA HUNTINGTON'S latest book of poetry, *Heavenly Bodies*, was the 2011 Editor's Selection in the Crab Orchard Poetry Series, Southern Illinois University Press. She lives in Vermont and teaches at Dartmouth College.

DANIEL JOHNSON published *How to Catch a Falling Knife*, his first book of poetry, with Alice James Books in 2010. In conjunction with the book's release, he has been performing an illuminated version of the manuscript involving original music and the found home movies of William Bradley, a World War II-era Fuller Brush salesman from Davenport, Iowa. Johnson is the founding executive director of 826 Boston, a nonprofit youth writing center, and he lives with his wife and daughter in Boston. To read more, visit www.danielbjohnson.com.

LINNEA JOHNSON grew up in Chicago and loves it still. She holds a BA and a PhD in English, and an MA in Writing and Women's Studies; she has taught in colleges and universities. She is also a watercolorist, photographer, fiction writer, and political activist. *Augury*, published December 2010, is Johnson's second full-length collection of poems. Her first collection, *The Chicago Home*, won the first Alice James Books Beatrice Hawley Award; first published in 1986, it was republished in 2007.

ALICE JONES is the winner of the Beatrice Hawley and Jane Kenyon Awards from Alice James Books. Her recent books include *Extreme Directions*, *Gorgeous Mourning*, and *Plunge*. Awards include the Lyric Poetry and Winner awards from the Poetry Society of America, the first

Narrative Magazine Poetry Award, and fellowships from the Bread Loaf Writers' Conference and the National Endowment for the Arts. She is a psychoanalyst practicing and teaching in Berkeley, and is the co-editor of Apogee Press.

JANET KAPLAN's three books are *The Groundnote*, *The Glazier's Country*, and *Dreamlife of a Philanthropist*, winner of the Sandeen Prize from University of Notre Dame Press. The recipient of fellowships and grants from New York Foundation for the Arts, Rattapallax, and the Vogelstein Foundation, Kaplan has also been a Fellow at Vermont Studio Center, Virginia Center for the Creative Arts, Ucross, and Yaddo. She is the publisher and editor of Red Glass Books and teaches at Hofstra University.

LAURA KASISCHKE has published eight collections of poetry and eight novels. For her most recent collection, *Space, in Chains*, she received the National Book Critics Circle Award. She lives with her family in Chelsea, Michigan.

CLAUDIA KEELAN's most recent book is *Missing Her* from New Issues Press.

*JANE KENYON (1947–1995) received her MA in English Language and Literature from the University of Michigan. In 1975 she moved with her husband, Donald Hall, to his family's nineteenth century farmhouse in New Hampshire. *From Room to Room* was her first book, published by Alice James Books in 1978. She was an active member of the Alice James Poetry Cooperative and a supporter for many years. Kenyon authored four other collections: *The Boat of Quiet Hours* (Graywolf Press, 1986), *Constance* (1993), *Let Evening Come* (1990), and *Otherwise: New and Selected Poems* (1997). *Hundred White Daffodils*, a collection of Kenyon's prose and poetry, was published posthumously by Graywolf Press in 2000.

ANN KILLOUGH's poems have appeared in *Fence*, *Field*, *Mudfish*, *Poetry Ireland*, *Salamander*, *Sentence*, and elsewhere. Her chapbook *Sinners in the Hands: Selections from the Catalog* won the 2003 Robert Phillips Poetry Chapbook Prize from Texas Review Press; her book *Beloved Idea*, published by Alice James Books in October 2007, won the 2008 L.L. Winship/ PEN New England Poetry Award. She is a co-director of the Brookline Poetry Series in Brookline, Massachusetts.

DAVID KIRBY is the author of numerous books, including *The House on Boulevard St.: New and Selected Poems*, a finalist for the 2007 National Book Award. His biography, *Little Richard: The Birth of Rock 'n' Roll*, was hailed by *The Times Literary Supplement of London* as a "hymn of praise to the emancipatory power of nonsense." He is the Robert O. Lawton Distinguished Professor of English at Florida State University. See also www.davidkirby.com.

ELIZABETH KNIES is the author of *The New Year and Other Poems* and *Streets After Rain*, both published by Alice James Books; *From the Window*, Teal Press; *White Peonies* and *Going and Coming Back*, Oyster River Press. She taught ESL, writing, critical thinking and literature in New Hampshire, Maine, Japan, Missouri, Colorado, and Massachusetts, and has worked as a reviewer and an editor. She lives in Portsmouth, New Hampshire.

SHARON KRAUS's books are *Generation* and *Strange Land* (University of Florida Press, 2001); her work has appeared in *Denver Quarterly*, *DIAGRAM*, *Quarterly West*, *Drunken Boat*, slope.com, and elsewhere. She is the poetry editor at Literary Mama (www.literarymama.com).

Former U.S. Poet Laureate, MAXINE KUMIN, winner of the Pulitzer and Ruth Lilly prizes, is the author of *Where I Live: New & Selected Poems 1990-2010* (Norton), her seventeenth volume, which won the 2011 L.A. Times Poetry Book Prize. She has taught at MIT, Brandeis, Princeton, Columbia, Washington University of St. Louis, and served on the Bread Loaf Writers' Conference faculty for seven years. She and her husband live on a farm in New Hampshire.

NANCY LAGOMARSINO is the author of three books of prose poetry, *Sleep Handbook* (Alice James Books, 1987), *The Secretary Parables* (Alice James Books, 1991), and *Light from an Eclipse* (White Pine Press, 2005). She was born in Montpelier, Vermont, earned an MFA in Creative Writing from Vermont College, and has lived in Hanover, New Hampshire since 1974.

RUTH LEPSON is poet-in-residence at the New England Conservatory. Her books are *Dreaming in Color* (Alice James Books), *Morphology*, and *I Went Looking for You* (both from BlazeVOX), and the forthcoming *Box* (Pressed Wafer). She edited *Poetry from Sojourner: A Feminist Anthology* (University of Illinois Press). Her poems have appeared in *EOAGH*, *Big Bridge*, *AGNI*, *Boog City*, and many other publications. She collaborates with musicians and performs with them in New York and Massachusetts.

LESLE LEWIS's books include *Small Boat* (winner of the 2002 Iowa Poetry Prize), *Landscapes I & II* (Alice James Books, 2006) and *lie down too* (Alice James Books, 2011). She's had poems in many journals, including *American Letters and Commentary*, *Northern New England Review*, *Hotel Amerika*, *Mississippi Review*, *The Cincinnati Review*, *Green Mountains Review*, *Barrow Street*, *Mudfish*, *LIT*, *Pool*, *jubilat*, *notnostrums*, and *Sentence*. Lesle Lewis lives in New Hampshire and is a Professor of English at Landmark College.

KAREN LINDSEY is an adjunct at Emerson College and the University of Massachusetts Boston. Her book about Henry VIII's wives, *Divorced, Beheaded, Survived*, was published by Perseus. She is a co-author, with Dr. Susan Love, of all editions of *Dr. Susan Love's Breast Book*, *Dr. Susan Love's Hormone Book*, and with Dr. Daniel Tobin of *Peaceful Dying* and *That Silver-Haired Daddy of Mine*. Her blog site is "Anything&Everything" (waroomniet.blogspot.com).

TIMOTHY LIU is the author of eight books of poems, most recently *Bending the Mind Around the Dream's Blown Fuse*. His poems have been translated into ten languages, and his journals and papers are archived in the Berg Collection at the New York Public Library. *Vox Angelica* received the 1992

Norma Farber First Book Award from the Poetry Society of America (judged by Carolyn Forche). Liu lives in Manhattan with his husband.

MARGARET LLOYD'S *This Particular Earthly Scene* was published by Alice James Books in 1993 and Plinth Books published her *A Moment in the Field: Voices from Arthurian Legend* in 2006. Her poetry awards and prizes include a National Endowment for the Humanities grant, a fellowship to Hawthornden Castle in Scotland, and a writing residency at Yaddo where she worked on her forthcoming collection of poems, *The Cows of Heaven.* Lloyd chairs the Humanities Department at Springfield College, Massachusetts.

MARGO LOCKWOOD, a secondhand bookdealer and gallery owner in Brookline and Boston since 1962, started publishing poets in 1963, and began being published herself in 1972 when an undergraduate student at the University of Massachusetts Boston. She studied with Ron Schreiber, a founding member of Alice James Books. Widowed at 30 with four children, she lived two separate years in Dublin, Ireland and found terrorism and the Irish climate equally bracing and daunting. She has had eight books of poetry published, two with Alice James Books, and is in several anthologies. Her memoir, *A Virgin in Whiskey Point*, will soon be in print.

SABRA LOOMIS's book, *House Held Together by Winds* (Harper Perennial, 2008), was a winner of the 2007 National Poetry Series open competition, as selected by James Tate. A book of poems, *Rosetree*, was published by Alice James Books in 1989. Speaking of her poem "The Alphabet of Singing," Eamon Grennan has said, "Resisting rational paraphrase or narrative explication, it seems to utter itself from the center of a rapt consciousness, making its own kind of lyrical sense."

ALESSANDRA LYNCH is the author of two collections of poetry, *Sails the Wind Left Behind* (2002) and *It Was a Terrible Cloud at Twilight* (2008). Her poems have appeared in *The American Poetry Review, Crazyhorse, jubilat, The Massachusetts Review, Ploughshares, Virginia Quarterly Review,* and other journals. She has had residencies at The MacDowell Colony and Yaddo. Alessandra lives near an Indianapolisian canal and teaches at Butler University.

SARAH MANGUSO is the author of the book-length essays *The Guardians* (2012) and *The Two Kinds of Decay* (2008), the story collection *Hard to Admit and Harder to Escape* (2007), and the poetry collections *Siste Viator* (2006) and *The Captain Lands in Paradise* (2002). Honors for her writing include a Guggenheim Fellowship and the Rome Prize. She lives in Brooklyn, New York.

ADRIAN MATEJKA is the author of *The Devil's Garden* (Alice James Books, 2003), *Mixology* (Penguin USA, 2009), and *The Big Smoke* (Penguin USA, forthcoming in 2013). He is the recipient of two Illinois Arts Council Literary Awards and fellowships from Cave Canem and the Lannan Foundation. His work has appeared or is forthcoming in *The American Poetry Review*, *The Best American Poetry 2010*, *Ploughshares*, and *Poetry* among other journals and anthologies.

SUZANNE MATSON is the author of two volumes of poetry, *Durable Goods* and *Sea Level*, from Alice James Books. A 2012 recipient of a National Endowment for the Arts Fellowship in Fiction, she is also the author of three novels, most recently *The Tree-Sitter*, all from W. W. Norton. She is a professor at Boston College and also teaches in the low-residency MFA program at Fairfield University.

ALICE MATTISON'S book of poems, *Animals*, was published by Alice James Books in 1980. She is the author of ten novels and story collections, most recently the novel *When We Argued All Night*. Her stories and essays have appeared in many publications, including *The New Yorker*, *The New York Times*, *The Threepenny Review*, *Ploughshares*, and *Ecotone*, and have been anthologized in *The Pushcart Prize*, *The PEN: O.Henry Prize Stories*, and *Best American Short Stories*.

SHARA MCCALLUM is the author of four books of poetry: *The Face of Water: New and Selected Poems*, *This Strange Land*, *Song of Thieves*, and *The Water Between Us*. Her poems have appeared in journals, anthologies, and textbooks in the U.S., U.K., Caribbean, Latin America, and Israel and have been translated into Spanish and Romanian. Originally from Jamaica, she lives with her family in Pennsylvania, where she directs the Stadler Center for Poetry and teaches at Bucknell University.

LAURA MCCULLOUGH'S most recent books are *Panic*, winner of the Kinereth Genseler Award from Alice James Books and *Speech Acts* from Black Lawrence Press, which will also publish her next book, *Rigger Death & Hoist Another* in February 2013. Her poems, essays, fiction, and interviews have appeared in *The American Poetry Review*, *New South*, *Green Mountains Review*, *Pebble Lake Review*, *Georgia Review*, *The Writer's Chronicle*, and others. She is the editor of *An Integrity of Aloneness: On the Poetry of Stephen Dunn*, forthcoming fall 2013 from University of Syracuse Press and is editing *The Task of Un/Masking: Essays on Poetry and Race*. She is also editor-at-large for *Trans-Portal* magazine.

Poet, nonfiction writer DAVID MCKAIN is Professor Emeritus at the University of Connecticut. Before teaching, he worked as an editor at McGraw Hill and Holt Rinehart and Winston. His books include *Spellbound: Growing up in God's Country* (memoir, 1989), *In Touch* (Ardis, 1975), *The Common Life* (Alice James Books, 1982), and *Spirit Bodies* (Ithaka House, 1990)—the latter, all collections of poetry. He also edited *The Whole Earth: Essays in Appreciation, Anger, and Hope* (1971) and *Christianity: Some Non-Christian Appraisals* (1965). *Spellbound* was the winner of the Associated Writing Programs Award for creative nonfiction in 1989. He lives in Preston, Connecticut with his wife Margaret Gibson.

JANE MEAD is the recipient of grants and awards from the Guggenheim, Lannan, and Whiting Foundations. Her third book, *The Usable Field*, was published by Alice James Books in 2008. For many years a Poet-in-Residence at Wake Forest University, she now teaches in the Low-Residency MFA Program in Poetry at Drew University, and farms her grandfather's vineyard in Northern California.

HELENA MINTON is the author of two books with Alice James Books, *Personal Effects*, with Robin Becker and Marilyn Zuckerman, and *The Canal Bed*. Her most recent collection, *The Gardener and the Bees*, was published by March Street Press. Her poems have appeared in a variety of journals and anthologies, including *Solstice*, *Parting Gifts*, *edna*, and *Sojourner: A Feminist Anthology*. She works as a librarian near Boston.

NORA MITCHELL has published two books, *Your Skin Is A Country* and *Proofreading the Histories,* with Alice James Books. Her poems have also been published in journals such as *Green Mountains Review, Hunger Mountain,* and *Ploughshares* and anthologized in *Onion River: Six Vermont Poets* (1997) and *Contemporary Poets of New England* (2002). She wrote and produced "Minus Music," a performance poem for four voices that played at Burlington's FlynnSpace, Goddard College, and St. Michael's College in 2003. She teaches writing and literature at Burlington College.

MIHAELA MOSCALIUC's poems, reviews, translations, and articles appear in *Georgia Review, Prairie Schooner, TriQuarterly, New Letters, Poetry International, Arts & Letters, Pleiades, Connecticut Review, Interculturality and Translation,* and *Orient and Orientalisms* in *American Poetry and Poetics.* She teaches in the Low-Residency MFA Program in Poetry and Poetry in Translation at Drew University and at Monmouth University.

STEPHEN MOTIKA's first book, *Western Practice,* was published by Alice James Books in 2012. He is also the editor of *Tiresias: The Collected Poems of Leland Hickman* (2009) and the author of the poetry chapbooks, *Arrival and at Mono* (2007) and *In the Madrones* (2011). A 2010-2011 Lower Manhattan Cultural Council Workspace Resident, he is the program director at Poets House and the publisher of Nightboat Books.

AMY NEWMAN is the author of *Order, or Disorder; Camera Lyrica; fall;* and *Dear Editor.* She teaches at Northern Illinois University.

IDRA NOVEY is the author of *Exit, Civilian,* a 2011 National Poetry Series selection, and *The Next Country.* She's received awards from the Poetry Society of America, the National Endowment for the Arts, and the PEN Translation Fund. Her recent translations include Clarice Lispector's novel *The Passion According to G.H.* forthcoming from New Directions and Penguin UK. She's taught in the Bard College Prison Initiative, at NYU, and in Columbia University's School of the Arts.

CAROLE OLES has published seven books of poems, most recently *Waking Stone: Inventions on the Life of Harriet Hosmer*. Professor Emerita at California State University, Chico, she has also taught at the University of Massachusetts Boston, Hollins College, Bread Loaf Writers' Conference, and Bread Loaf School of English. Among her honors are a National Endowment for the Arts Fellowship, a Pushcart Prize, the Virginia Prize for Poetry, *Prairie Schooner* Awards, and The MacDowell Colony Fellowships.

JANINE OSHIRO graduated from Whitworth University, Portland State University, and the University of Iowa Writers' Workshop. A Kundiman fellow and winner of Hawaii's Elliot Cades Award for Literature, she lives in Hawaii and teaches at Windward Community College.

JEAN-PAUL PECQUEUR is a poet from the Pacific Northwest, who currently lives in Brooklyn. *The Case Against Happiness* was his first book.

*JEAN PEDRICK (1922–2006) was a founding member of the Alice James Poetry Cooperative. She is the author of *Wolf Moon, Pride & Splendor, Greenfellow*, and several chapbooks. Her final collection, *Catgut*, was published in 2003 by Pomme Press.

MATTHEW PENNOCK is the author of *Sudden Dog* (Alice James Books, 2012). His poems have appeared in such journals as *Western Humanities Review, Denver Quarterly, New York Quarterly, LIT*, and *Guernica: A Journal of Art and Politics*, among others. He lives in New York and teaches at Yeshiva University and New York City College of Technology.

JOYCE PESEROFF's four books of poems are *The Hardness Scale, A Dog in the Lifeboat, Mortal Education*, and *Eastern Mountain Time*. She is the editor of *Robert Bly: When Sleepers Awake, The Ploughshares Poetry Reader*, and, most recently, *Simply Lasting: Writers on Jane Kenyon*. She has received fellowships from the National Endowment for the Arts and the Massachusetts Artists Foundation, and a Pushcart Prize. Recent work has appeared in *Consequence, New Ohio Review, Ploughshares*, and *Salamander*.

She is Distinguished Lecturer at the University of Massachusetts Boston, where she directed the MFA Program for its first four years.

CAROL POTTER'S fourth book of poems, *Otherwise Obedient* (Red Hen Press, 2008), was a finalist in the 2008 Lambda Literary Awards, and her previous book, *The Short History of Pets*, won the CSU Poetry Center Prize in 1999. Publications include poems in *Field*, *Poetry*, *The Iowa Review*, *The American Poetry Review*, *The Massachusetts Review*, and in the *Pushcart Prize XXVI*. She teaches for the Antioch University Los Angeles MFA program, and lives in Vermont.

LIA PURPURA is the author of seven collections of essays, poems, and translations, including *On Looking* (a finalist for the National Book Critics Circle Award in nonfiction) and most recently, *Rough Likeness*. Her awards include a 2012 Guggenheim Foundation Fellowship, the National Endowment for the Arts and Fulbright Fellowships, and four Pushcart Prizes. Her work appears in *The New Yorker*, *The New Republic*, *Orion*, and *Paris Review*. She is Writer-in-Residence at Loyola University, Baltimore, Maryland and teaches in the Rainier Writing Workshop in Tacoma, Washington.

BILL RASMOVICZ is the author of *The World in Place of Itself* (Alice James Books, 2007), which won the New England Poetry Club's Shelia Margaret Motton Prize. His poems have appeared in *Hotel Amerika*, *Nimrod*, *Mid-American Review*, *Third Coast*, *Gulf Coast*, and other publications. Bill has served as a workshop co-leader and literary excursion leader throughout Switzerland, Italy, Croatia, Slovenia, Germany, England, Wales, and the Czech Republic. A graduate of the Vermont College of Fine Arts MFA in Writing program and Temple University School of Pharmacy, he lives in Brooklyn, New York.

DONALD REVELL is the author of eleven collections of poetry, most recently of *Tantivy* (2012) and *The Bitter Withy* (2009), both from Alice James Books. He has published five volumes of translations from the French, including Apollinaire's *Alcools* (Wesleyan), Rimbaud's

Illuminations and *A Season in Hell* (both from Omnidawn), and Laforgue's *Last Verses* (Omnidawn). His critical writings include *The Art of Attention* (Graywolf Press) and *Invisible Green: Selected Prose* (Omnidawn). Winner of the PEN USA Translation Award and two-time winner of the PEN USA Award for Poetry, he has also won the Academy of American Poets' Lenore Marshall Prize and is a former Fellow of the Ingram Merrill and Guggenheim Foundations. Additionally, he has twice been awarded fellowships from the National Endowment for the Arts. Former editor-in-chief of *Denver Quarterly*, he now serves as poetry editor of *Colorado Review*. Revell is a Professor of English and Creative Writing at the University of Nevada, Las Vegas.

LEE RUDOLPH is a mathematician: a knot-theorist who has recently applied topology to robotics and to social and cultural psychology. For his most recent book, *Qualitative Methods for the Social Sciences* (Routledge/Psychology Press, August 2012), he drew approximately 100 illustrative figures, edited eight contributed chapters, and wrote four chapters of his own. The title poem of his previous book, "A Woman and a Man, Ice-Fishing" (Texas Review Press, 2006), originally appeared in *The New Yorker*.

CHERYL SAVAGEAU'S most recent book of poetry is *Mother/Land*. She has won fellowships in poetry from the National Endowment for the Arts and the Massachusetts Artists Foundation. Her work is widely anthologized. Savageau has taught at Holy Cross College, Clark University, the University of New Mexico, the University of Massachusetts Amherst, the University of New Hampshire, and in the Goddard College MFA program. Her textile work, paintings, and assemblages have been exhibited at the Abbe Museum in Bar Harbor, Maine.

WILLA SCHNEBERG was a member of Alice James in the early days in Cambridge. Her other collections are: *In The Margins Of The World*, winner of the Oregon Book Award for Poetry, and *Storytelling in Cambodia*. Poems appeared in *The American Poetry Review*, *Salmagundi*, *Women's Review of Books*, *Poet Lore*, and *I Go To The Ruined Place: Contemporary Poems in*

Defense of Global Human Rights. Willa is a social worker in private practice and a visual artist.

*RON SCHREIBER (1934–2004) was a founding member of the Alice James Poetry Cooperative. He is the author of several poetry collections, including *John: Poems* (Hanging Loose Press, 1989). Schreiber taught at the University of Massachusetts Boston for more than three decades.

After AJB, two roads diverged, and JEFFREY SCHWARTZ took both. One led to poetry, which he still writes and publishes. The other led to composition and rhetoric. Along this path, he has written widely for journals and books on technology, film, interdisciplinary studies, and student-centered learning. For 24 years, he has worked at a girls school with young writers who collaborate a la AJB on a magazine that has won many awards. He lives in Fairfield, Connecticut with his wife Betsy, son Ben, and dog Finne.

LISA SEWELL is the author of *The Way Out, Name Withheld*, and *Long Corridor*, which won the 2009 Keystone Chapbook Award. She is also co-editor with Claudia Rankine of *American Poets in the 21ˢᵗ Century: The New Poetics* and *Eleven More American Women Poets in the 21ˢᵗ Century: Poetics Across North America*. She has received grants and awards from the Leeway Foundation, the Pennsylvania Council for the Arts, and the National Endowment for the Arts. She lives in Philadelphia and teaches at Villanova University.

BETSY SHOLL'S most recent book of poetry is *Rough Cradle* (Alice James Books). From 2006 to 2011 she served as Poet Laureate of Maine. Recent poems have or will appear in *Ploughshares, Image, Field, Brilliant Corners, The Massachusetts Review*, and *Best Spiritual Writing 2012*. She teaches in the MFA program of Vermont College of Fine Arts.

SUSAN SNIVELY is the author of four books of poetry: *From This Distance* (Alice James Books, 1981), *Voices in the House* (University of

Alabama Poetry Series, 1988), *The Undertow* (University of Central Florida Contemporary Poetry Series, 1998), and *Skeptic Traveler* (David Robert Books, 2005). Snively, who grew up in Louisville, Kentucky, has published poems most recently in *Prairie Schooner*, *The Southern Humanities Review*, *Spoon River Poetry Review*, *The Florida Review*, *The Vocabula Review*, and *Antioch Review*. She has also published essays in *The Southern Review*, *storySouth*, *The Florida Review*, and *Tampa Review*. She has taught at Smith College, Mount Holyoke College, and Amherst College, and has received fellowships from the National Endowment for the Arts and the Massachusetts Artists Foundation.

JANE SPRINGER is the author of *Dear Blackbird* (Agha Shahid Ali Prize, 2007) and *Murder Ballad* (Alice James Books, 2012). Her honors include a Pushcart Prize, a National Endowment for the Arts Fellowship and a Whiting Writers' Award. She lives in upstate New York with her husband, their son, and their two dogs, Walter Woofus and Maple.

SUE STANDING's collections of poems include *Deception Pass*, *Gravida*, and *False Horizon*. She teaches at Wheaton College in Massachusetts.

ADRIENNE SU, whose first book, *Middle Kingdom*, was published by Alice James Books in 1997, is poet-in-residence at Dickinson College in Pennsylvania. Among her awards are a National Endowment for the Arts Fellowship, a Pushcart Prize, and inclusion in *Best American Poetry*. Her subsequent books are *Sanctuary* (Manic D Press, 2006) and *Having None of It* (2009).

CHAD SWEENEY is the author of four books of poetry, most recently *Parable of Hide and Seek* (Alice James Books) and *Wolf's Milk: Lost Notebooks of Juan Sweeney*. His poems have been selected for both *Best American Poetry* and *The Pushcart Prize Anthology*. He is co-translator of the selected poems of Iranian poet H. E. Sayeh. Sweeney holds a PhD from Western Michigan University and teaches in the MFA program at California State University, San Bernardino.

Cole Swensen is the author of fourteen volumes of poetry, most recently *Gravesend* (University of California, 2012), and a collection of critical essays. *Goest* (Alice James Books, 2004) was a finalist for the National Book Award, and other volumes have won the National Poetry Series, the Iowa Poetry Prize, and the S.F. State Poetry Center Book Award. Co-editor of the 2009 Norton anthology *American Hybrid* and founding editor of La Presse Books, she teaches at Brown University.

Larissa Szporluk is the author of five books of poetry. Recent poems have appeared in *Ploughshares* and *Burnside Review*. Her new book, *Traffic with Macbeth*, was published in 2011 by Tupelo Press. The recipient of a 2009 Guggenheim Fellowship in Poetry, she teaches creative writing at Bowling Green State University in Bowling Green, Ohio.

Mary Szybist is the author of two collections of poetry: *Granted*, which won the Beatrice Hawley Award from Alice James Books in 2003 and was a finalist for the National Book Critics Circle Award, and *Incarnadine* (Graywolf Press, 2013). She lives in Portland, Oregon with her husband Jerry Harp and teaches at Lewis & Clark College and the Warren Wilson MFA program.

Tom Thompson is the author of *Live Feed* and *The Pitch*, both published by Alice James Books. His poems, essays, and reviews have appeared in many journals including *Boston Review*, *Colorado Review*, *Conduit*, and *Post Road*, as well as online at poets.org and fishousepoems.org. He lives in New York City with his family, and works at an advertising agency. Learn more at tthompson.net.

Brian Turner (author of *Here, Bullet* and *Phantom Noise*) received a USA Hillcrest Fellowship in Literature, a National Endowment for the Arts Literature Fellowship in Poetry, the Amy Lowell Traveling Fellowship, the US-Japan Friendship Commission grant, the Poets' Prize, and a fellowship from the Lannan Foundation. His work has appeared on National Public Radio, the BBC, *Newshour* with Jim Lehrer, and *Weekend America*, among others. He is the director of the low-residency MFA program at Sierra Nevada College.

Jean Valentine is the author of eleven books of poetry, including *Break the Glass*, published by Copper Canyon Press in 2010. She is a co-translator with Ilya Kaminsky of *Dark Elderberry Branch: Poems of Marina Tsvetaeva*, published by Alice James Books in 2012. She lives and works in New York City.

Cornelia Veenendaal has published poems in various magazines, among them *Commonweal, Hanging Loose, Off the Coast, Prairie Schooner*, and *Sojourner*. She has written three volumes of poetry. After teaching literature and writing at the University of Massachusetts Boston for twenty-five years, she is retired, lives and writes in Dorchester, and meets regularly with nearby Alice James poets to read and talk about new work.

Liz Waldner's first published book was *Homing Devices*, published by O Books in 1998. Her most recent, though not last, book was *Play*, published by Lightful Press in 2009. Her penultimate book, *Trust*, (Cleveland State University Poetry Center, 2008) was actually her second book. Her first has never been published and her last two are apparently going through the mandatory aging process. As is she, being, all unlikely, still alive.

Peter Waldor is the author of *Door to a Noisy Room* (Alice James Books, 2008) which was a finalist for the 2009 National Jewish Book Award. His book, *At the Last Split Second* is due out in December of 2012 from Settlement House. His book-length poem *Leg Paint* appeared in the online magazine *Mudlark* (the poems are the subject of an in process poetry-painting collaboration with the painter Nancy Ring). His work has appeared in many journals, including *The American Poetry Review, Ploughshares, The Iowa Review, Colorado Review, Poetry Daily, Verse Daily*, and *Mothering Magazine*. Waldor works in the insurance business and lives in northern New Jersey.

After a long haul editing magazines and co-authoring eight book collaborations, Larkin Warren is at last calling her own bluff on her memoir, as well as the poetry manuscript for which she received an NEA grant in the mid-1980s. She lives in a log cabin in the Connecticut woods with a newspaper reporter, a coyote-obsessed golden retriever, and occasionally a very tall ice-cream consuming grandson. She shouts out to dear Joycie and raises a glass to the abiding spirit of Jane, for whom she is ever grateful.

ELLEN DORÉ WATSON'S most recent book is *Dogged Hearts*. Individual poems have appeared widely, including in *Tin House*, *Orion*, and *The New Yorker*. Among her honors are a Rona Jaffe Writers Award and fellowships to The MacDowell Colony and to Yaddo. Watson teaches creative writing and directs the Poetry Center at Smith College, serves as an editor of *The Massachusetts Review, and* teaches in the Drew University Low-Residency MFA Program in Poetry and Translation.

DAVID WILLIAMS is the author of two poetry collections, *Traveling Mercies* and *Far Sides of the Only World*. His work has appeared in dozens of magazines, most recently in *Image*, *Orion*, *Ploughshares*, *Prairie Schooner*, and *World Literature Today*, and eight anthologies, including *Post-Gibran: New Arab-American Writing* and *Dinarzad's Children: Contemporary Arab-American Fiction*. His writing is discussed at length in *Memory and Cultural Politics: New Ethnic American Literatures*.

SUZANNE WISE is the author of the poetry collection *The Kingdom of the Subjunctive*. Her poetry can also be found in *Legitimate Dangers: American Poets of the New Century* and in recent issues of *American Letters & Commentary*, *Ploughshares*, *Bone Bouquet*, *Catch Up*, *Green Mountains Review*, *Guernica*, and *Quarter After Eight*. She has taught creative writing at Pratt Institute, Middlebury College, and the University of Michigan. She lives in Brooklyn, New York.

JON WOODWARD'S books are *Uncanny Valley* (Cleveland State University Poetry Center), *Rain* (Wave Books), and *Mister Goodbye Easter Island* (Alice James Books). He lives in Boston with his wife, poet and pianist Oni Buchanan, and he works at the Harvard Museum of Comparative Zoology. His website is jonwoodward.net.

MARILYN ZUCKERMAN published five books of poetry: *Personal Effects* (Alice James Books), *Monday Morning Movie* (Street Editions), *Poems of the Sixth Decade* (Garden Street Press), *America/America* (Cedar Hill Publications), and *In the Ninth Decade* (Red Dragonfly Press), as well as a chapbook from The Greatest Hits series, Pudding House Publications in 2001. Zuckerman has received a PEN Syndicated Fiction Award and an Allen Ginsberg Poetry Award.

CREDITS

ALICE JAMES BOOKS *has made every effort to locate authors published in this anthology. If we have overlooked anyone, please contact us so we can correct our records at the next opportunity.*

AUTHOR INDEX

TITLE INDEX

BOOK BENEFACTORS

Alice James Books wishes to thank the following individuals,
who generously contributed toward the publication of *Lit from Inside:
40 Years of Poetry from Alice James Books*:

Book Benefactors

Nina Nyhart
Linnea Johnson
In loving memory of Joseph Salerno
Brian Turner
Cornelia Veenendaal
In memory of Max Kaden

Additional Contributors:

Daniel Gensler

For more information about AJB's book benefactor program, contact us
via phone or email, or visit us at www.alicejamesbooks.org to see a list of
forthcoming titles.

RECENT TITLES FROM ALICE JAMES BOOKS

Black Crow Dress, Roxane Beth Johnson
Dark Elderberry Branch: Poems of Marina Tsvetaeva, A Reading by
    Ilya Kaminsky and Jean Valentine
Tantivy, Donald Revell
Murder Ballad, Jane Springer
Sudden Dog, Matthew Pennock
Western Practice, Stephen Motika
me and Nina, Monica A. Hand
Hagar Before the Occupation | Hagar After the Occupation, Amal al-Jubouri
Pier, Janine Oshiro
Heart First into the Forest, Stacy Gnall
This Strange Land, Shara McCallum
lie down too, Lesle Lewis
Panic, Laura McCullough
Milk Dress, Nicole Cooley
Parable of Hide and Seek, Chad Sweeney
Shahid Reads His Own Palm, Reginald Dwayne Betts
How to Catch a Falling Knife, Daniel Johnson
Phantom Noise, Brian Turner
Father Dirt, Mihaela Moscaliuc
Pageant, Joanna Fuhrman
The Bitter Withy, Donald Revell
Winter Tenor, Kevin Goodan
Slamming Open the Door, Kathleen Sheeder Bonanno
Rough Cradle, Betsy Sholl
Shelter, Carey Salerno
The Next Country, Idra Novey
Begin Anywhere, Frank Giampietro
The Usable Field, Jane Mead
King Baby, Lia Purpura
The Temple Gate Called Beautiful, David Kirby
Door to a Noisy Room, Peter Waldor

Alice James Books has been publishing poetry since 1973 and remains one of the few presses in the country that is run collectively. The cooperative selects manuscripts for publication primarily through regional and national annual competitions. Authors who win a Kinereth Gensler Award become active members of the cooperative board and participate in the editorial decisions of the press. The press, which historically has placed an emphasis on publishing women poets, was named for Alice James, sister of William and Henry, whose fine journal and gift for writing went unrecognized during her lifetime.

Designed by Mary Austin Speaker

Printed by Thompson-Shore
on 30% postconsumer recycled paper
processed chlorine-free